McDougal Littell

Biology

Study Guide

McDougal Littell
A HOUGHTON MIFFLIN COMPANY

Evanston, Illinois • **Boston** • **Dallas**

McDOUGAL LITTELL BIOLOGY
Study Guide Contents

UNIT 4 EVOLUTION

STUDY GUIDE CONTENTS, CONTINUED

SECTION 1.1 | THE STUDY OF LIFE
Study Guide

KEY CONCEPT
Biologists study life in all its forms.

<table>
<tr><td colspan="3">VOCABULARY</td></tr>
<tr><td>biosphere</td><td>biology</td><td>metabolism</td></tr>
<tr><td>biodiversity</td><td>organism</td><td>DNA</td></tr>
<tr><td>species</td><td>cell</td><td></td></tr>
</table>

MAIN IDEA: **Earth is home to an incredible diversity of life.**
Take notes about the diversity of life on Earth in the chart below.

1. In the box labeled **The Biosphere,** list examples of environments on earth in which life is found.

2. In the box labeled **Biodiversity,** write a definition of the term in your own words.

3. In the box labeled **Species,** briefly explain what a species is.

> **Earth is home to an incredible diversity of life.**
>
> **The Biosphere**
>
> **Biodiversity**
>
> **Species**

4. How is biodiversity related to the biosphere?

_____

_____

5. In general, how does biodiversity vary across the biosphere?

_____

_____

MAIN IDEA: **All organisms share certain characteristics.**

6. Before reading, take a quick look at the headings in this main idea. What are the four characteristics that identify something as living?

_____

7. As you read, take notes on how the four basic characteristics help define what is a living thing.

Characteristic	Summary Sentence
Cells	
Energy and metabolism	
Response to environment	
Reproduction and development	

Vocabulary Check

8. The word *biosphere* is made up of two word parts: *bio-* and *sphere*. How can these two word parts help you to remember the definition of biosphere?

_____

_____

9. What is an organism?

_____

10. The term *metabolism* is based on a Greek word that means "change." How is this meaning related to the meaning of metabolism?

_____

11. How is DNA related to reproduction?

_____

SECTION
1.2

UNIFYING THEMES OF BIOLOGY
Study Guide

KEY CONCEPT
Unifying themes connect concepts from many fields of biology.

VOCABULARY		
system	homeostasis	adaptation
ecosystem	evolution	

MAIN IDEA: All levels of life have systems of related parts.

1. What is a system?

_____

_____

2. What are some examples of systems?

_____

_____

Complete the table by writing either the level of life or an example of a system at that level of life.

Level	Example
3.	Chemicals and processes interact in a precise way so that a cell can function properly.
Cells	**4.**
5.	Different parts of a living thing work together so that the living thing can survive.
Ecosystem	**6.**

MAIN IDEA: Structure and function are related in biology.

7. What are structure and function?

_____

_____

8. Give an example of how structure and function are related on the cellular level.

_____

_____

Section 1.2 STUDY GUIDE CONTINUED

CHAPTER 1
Biology in the 21st Century

MAIN IDEA: **Organisms must maintain homeostasis to survive in diverse environments.**

9. What is homeostasis?

_____

10. Why is homeostasis important to the survival of an organism?

_____

_____

11. In the space below, draw a sketch to help you remember what negative feedback is.

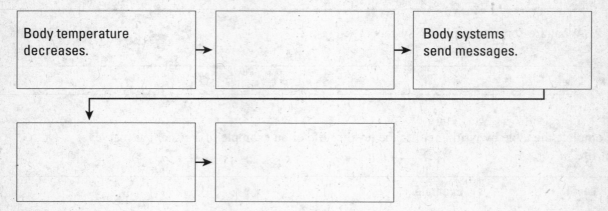

MAIN IDEA: **Evolution explains the unity and diversity of life.**

12. What is evolution?

_____

13. Over the course of time, evolution _____ the genetic makeup of a population.

14. _____ are genetic traits that give an advantage to an individual and can be passed on to offspring.

Vocabulary Check

15. A system in which living and nonliving things in a certain area interact is called a(n)

_____.

16. The maintenance of constant internal conditions in an organism is called

_____.

SECTION 1.3 | SCIENTIFIC THINKING AND PROCESSES
Study Guide

KEY CONCEPT
Science is a way of thinking, questioning, and gathering evidence.

VOCABULARY			
observation	hypothesis	independent variable	constant
data	experiment	dependent variable	theory

MAIN IDEA: Like all science, biology is a process of inquiry.

Complete the table below by giving a brief description and a brief example of each of the scientific process terms.

Scientific Process	Description	Example
Observation	1.	2.
Data	3.	4.
Hypothesis	5.	6.

7. How do scientists use statistics when they test a hypothesis?

_____

_____

8. Why is it important that a scientist's results are evaluated by other scientists?

_____

_____

Section 1.3 STUDY GUIDE CONTINUED

9. Look at Figure 1.10. Beginning with observation, what are the five parts of scientific thinking?

_____

_____

MAIN IDEA: **Biologists use experiments to test hypotheses.**

10. In _____ studies, scientists do not interfere with what is going on.

11. Scientists can test hypotheses through _____ .

12. A(n) _____ variable is one which is observed and not manipulated by the scientist.

13. How are constants different from independent variables?

_____

_____

MAIN IDEA: **A theory explains a wide range of observations.**

14. What is the difference between a theory and a hypothesis?

_____

15. Why are theories never proven?

_____

Vocabulary Check

16. What is a hypothesis?

_____

17. How can you remember the difference between an independent variable and a dependent variable? Think about what the words *independent* and *dependent* mean.

_____

_____

_____

SECTION
1.4 | BIOLOGISTS' TOOLS AND TECHNOLOGY
Study Guide

KEY CONCEPT
Technology continually changes the way biologists work.

VOCABULARY	
microscope	molecular genetics
gene	genomics

MAIN IDEA: Imaging technologies provide new views of life.

Compare and contrast the different types of microscopes and medical imaging techniques.

Type of Technology	Characteristics
Light microscope (LM)	**1.**
Scanning electron microscope (SEM)	**2.**
Transmission electron microscope (TEM)	**3.**
X-ray	**4.**
Magnetic resonance imaging (MRI)	**5.**

Section 1.4 STUDY GUIDE CONTINUED

MAIN IDEA: **Complex systems are modeled on computers.**

6. What is a model?

_____

_____

7. Why might scientists use computer models in research instead of conducting an experiment on the real system they would like to study?

_____

_____

MAIN IDEA: **The tools of molecular genetics give rise to new biological studies.**

8. What is a gene?

_____

9. How are computers used in genomics?

_____

_____

10. How does a gene differ from a genome?

_____

Vocabulary Check

11. The term *genomics* is related to the term *genome*. How does the definition of genome give you a clue about what genomics means?

_____

_____

12. The term *molecular genetics* is made up of two words: *molecular* and *genetics*. What are the meanings of these two words, and how can these words help you to remember what molecular genetics is?

_____

_____

SECTION
1.5

BIOLOGY AND YOUR FUTURE
Study Guide

KEY CONCEPT
Understanding biology can help you make informed decisions.

VOCABULARY
biotechnology
transgenic

MAIN IDEA: **Your health and the health of the environment depend on your knowledge of biology.**

1. Briefly describe three ways in which biology can help you make informed decisions about your health.

   _____

   _____

2. Briefly describe why biology and scientific thinking can help you make informed decisions related to the world around you.

   _____

   _____

MAIN IDEA: **Biotechnology offers great promise but also raises many issues.**

3. What is biotechnology?

   _____

Use the chart below to list the benefits of biotechnology, as well as the risks and ethical concerns about biotechnology.

Benefits	Risks and Ethical Concerns
4.	5.

Section 1.5 STUDY GUIDE CONTINUED

MAIN IDEA: Biology presents many unanswered questions.

6. Most of our knowledge about DNA was discovered during the past

_____ years.

7. Many questions go _____ because we don't know enough about

biology to even come up with those questions.

8. Before the invention of the microscope, people did not know about cells and bacteria.
With this in mind, why do you think many questions go unanswered and unasked?

_____

_____

Vocabulary Check

Each of the vocabulary words has been divided into its root words. Define the roots. Then
use the definitions to define the vocabulary word.

9. *Transgenic organism* can be divided into *trans-* and *genic*.

_____

_____

10. *Biotechnology* can be divided into *bio-* and *technology*.

_____

_____

Any Questions?

11. What questions do you have about biology or scientific research? List three topics in
biology that you want to learn more about, and why they interest you.

_____

_____

_____

_____

_____

_____

SECTION 2.1

ATOMS, IONS, AND MOLECULES

Study Guide

KEY CONCEPT
All living things are based on atoms and their interactions.

VOCABULARY		
atom	ion	molecule
element	ionic bond	
compound	covalent bond	

MAIN IDEA: Living things consist of atoms of different elements.

1. How are atoms and elements related?

_____

2. Sketch the structure of an atom. Label the protons, neutrons, nucleus, and electrons.

3. How do compounds differ from elements?

_____

MAIN IDEA: Ions form when atoms gain or lose electrons.

4. What is an ion?

_____

5. Why does an ion have an electrical charge?

_____

_____

Section 2.1 STUDY GUIDE CONTINUED

6. In the spaces provided below, sketch how both positive and negative ions form. Label the nucleus and the electrons. Use Figure 2.3 as a reference.

MAIN IDEA: Atoms share pairs of electrons in covalent bonds.

7. What is a covalent bond?

_____

8. What determines the number of covalent bonds that an atom can form?

_____

Vocabulary Check

element	compound	ion	molecule

_____ **9.** atoms held together by covalent bonds

_____ **10.** composed of different types of atoms

_____ **11.** composed of one type of atom

_____ **12.** atom that has gained or lost electrons

13. What is the difference between how ionic and covalent bonds form?

_____

_____

SECTION 2.2

PROPERTIES OF WATER
Study Guide

KEY CONCEPT

Water's unique properties allow life to exist on Earth.

VOCABULARY		
hydrogen bond	solution	acid
cohesion	solvent	base
adhesion	solute	pH

MAIN IDEA: Life depends on hydrogen bonds in water.

1. What is a polar molecule?

_____

2. Explain why water is a polar molecule.

_____

_____

3. What is a hydrogen bond?

_____

4. Describe where a hydrogen bond can form among water molecules.

_____

Complete the table by writing short descriptions about the properties of water.

Property	Description
High specific heat	5.
Cohesion	6.
Adhesion	7.

Section 2.2 STUDY GUIDE CONTINUED

MAIN IDEA: **Many compounds dissolve in water.**

8. What is the difference between a solvent and a solute?

_____

9. What types of substances dissolve easily in water?

_____

10. What types of substances do not dissolve easily in water?

_____

MAIN IDEA: **Some compounds form acids or bases.**

11. Take notes about the characteristics of acids and bases in the table below.

Characteristic	Acid	Base
Effect on H+ concentration in a solution		
Effect on pH		

Vocabulary Check

12. In the space below, sketch a solution using the Visual Vocab on page 42 as a reference. Label the solution, solvent, and solute. Next to these labels, write brief definitions for the terms.

SECTION 2.3
CARBON-BASED MOLECULES
Study Guide

KEY CONCEPT
Carbon-based molecules are the foundation of life.

VOCABULARY		
monomer	lipid	amino acid
polymer	fatty acid	nucleic acid
carbohydrate	protein	

MAIN IDEA: **Carbon atoms have unique bonding properties.**

1. Why is carbon often called the building block of life?

_____

_____

2. What ability allows carbon atoms to form a large number of molecules?

_____

_____

3. In the space below, sketch the three basic structures of carbon-based molecules: straight chain, branched chain, and ring.

Section 2.3 STUDY GUIDE CONTINUED

MAIN IDEA: **Four main types of carbon-based molecules are found in living things.**

Complete the table with functions and examples of each type of carbon-based molecule.

Molecule Type	Functions	Examples
Carbohydrate	4.	5.
Lipid	6.	7.
Protein	8.	9.
Nucleic acid	10.	11.

12. What determines a protein's structure and function?

_____

13. What are nucleic acids made of?

_____

Vocabulary Check

14. The prefix *mono-* means "one," and the prefix *poly-* means "many." How are these meanings related to the terms *monomer* and *polymer*?

_____

_____

_____

SECTION 2.4

CHEMICAL REACTIONS
Study Guide

KEY CONCEPT

Life depends on chemical reactions.

VOCABULARY		
chemical reaction	bond energy	exothermic
reactant	equilibrium	endothermic
product	activation energy	

MAIN IDEA: Bonds break and form during chemical reactions.

1. Label the reactants and products in the chemical reaction shown below. Write brief definitions for these terms next to their labels.

$$CH_4 + 2O_2 \longrightarrow CO_2 + 2H_2O$$

2. What causes chemical bonds to break during a reaction?

_____

3. What is bond energy?

_____

4. In a chemical equation, what symbol is used to show that a chemical reaction goes in both directions?

_____

5. When does a chemical reaction reach equilibrium?

_____

Section 2.4 STUDY GUIDE CONTINUED

MAIN IDEA: **Chemical reactions release or absorb energy.**

6. The _____ of the reactants and products determines whether

   energy will be released or absorbed during a chemical reaction.

7. Before a chemical reaction can start, _____ must be absorbed

   by the reactants. The amount that must be absorbed to start the reaction is called the

   _____ .

8. In an exothermic reaction, the products have a _____ bond

   energy than the reactants. Overall, energy is _____ .

9. In an endothermic reaction, the products have a _____ bond

   energy than the reactants. Overall, energy is _____ .

Vocabulary Check

10. Write one sentence that uses the words *chemical reaction, reactant,* and *product.*

   _____

11. Write your own analogy to remember the meaning of *activation energy.*

   _____

   _____

12. The term *equilibrium* is based on two Latin roots that mean "equal" and "balance." How
   do these meanings tell you the meaning of *equilibrium* in a chemical reaction?

   _____

   _____

13. The prefix *exo-* means "out," and the prefix *endo-* means "in." What do these prefixes
   tell you about *exothermic* and *endothermic* reactions?

   _____

   _____

SECTION
2.5

ENZYMES
Study Guide

KEY CONCEPT
Enzymes are catalysts for chemical reactions in living things.

VOCABULARY	
catalyst	substrate
enzyme	

MAIN IDEA: A catalyst lowers activation energy.

1. What is activation energy?

_____

_____

2. Take notes about catalysts in the chart below. In the first two boxes, write detail notes about the main functions of catalysts. In the third box, write a detail about another characteristic.

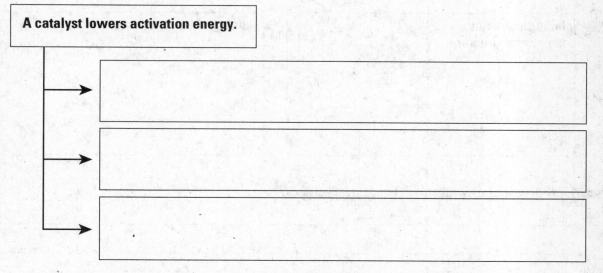

A catalyst lowers activation energy.

3. When a catalyst is present, more / less activation energy is needed to start a chemical reaction.

_____

Section 2.5 STUDY GUIDE CONTINUED

MAIN IDEA: Enzymes allow chemical reactions to occur under tightly controlled conditions.

4. Take notes about enzymes by filling in the Main Idea Web below.

Why enzymes are necessary:	How structure affects function:

Enzymes

Important factors in enzyme structure:	Lock-and-key model:

5. How do enzymes weaken the bonds in substrates?

_____

_____

Vocabulary Check

6. The word *catalyst* comes from the Greek word meaning "to dissolve." How does this definition relate to the meaning of *catalyst*?

_____

7. How are substrates like keys and enzymes like locks?

_____

_____

SECTION
3.1

CELL THEORY
Study Guide

KEY CONCEPT
Cells are the basic unit of life.

VOCABULARY		
cell theory	organelle	eukaryotic cell
cytoplasm	prokaryotic cell	

MAIN IDEA: Early studies led to the development of the cell theory.

In a phrase, tell what each scientist did to help develop the cell theory.

Scientist	Contribution to Cell Theory
1. Hooke	
2. Leeuwenhoek	
3. Schleiden	
4. Schwann	
5. Virchow	

6. What are the three parts of the cell theory?

_____

_____

_____

7. Give two reasons why the cell theory is important.

_____

_____

Section 3.1 STUDY GUIDE CONTINUED

CHAPTER 3
Cell Structure and Function

MAIN IDEA: **Prokaryotic cells lack a nucleus and most internal structures of eukaryotic cells.**

In the top left side of the Y shape below, write the characteristics of eukaryotic cells. In the top right side of the Y shape below, write the characteristics of prokaryotic cells. At the bottom of the Y shape below, write the characteristics that both kinds of cells have in common. Then lightly cross out those characteristics at the top of the Y.

Eukaryotic cells

_____

_____

_____

_____

Prokaryotic cells

_____

_____

_____

Both

_____

_____

_____

_____

Vocabulary Check

8. What is cytoplasm?

_____

9. Where do you find organelles?

_____

10. What statements summarize scientists' concepts of cells?

_____

11. Which type of cells have no nucleus?

_____

SECTION 3.2

CELL ORGANELLES
Study Guide

KEY CONCEPT
Eukaryotic cells share many similarities.

VOCABULARY		
cytoskeleton	Golgi apparatus	lysosome
nucleus	vesicle	centriole
endoplasmic reticulum	mitochondrion	cell wall
ribosome	vacuole	chloroplast

MAIN IDEA: **Cells have an internal structure.**

1. Look at Figure 3.5 in your textbook. What are the functions of a cytoskeleton?

_____

_____

2. How is a cytoskeleton like your skeleton?

_____

3. How is a cytoskeleton like your muscles?

_____

MAIN IDEA: **Several organelles are involved in making and processing proteins.**

Write either the function or the name of each organelle. Draw a sketch to help you remember it.

Organelle	Function	Sketch
4. nucleus		
5.	helps in the production of proteins and lipids	
6. ribosomes		
7. Golgi apparatus		
8.	carries certain molecules from place to place within a cell	

Section 3.2 STUDY GUIDE CONTINUED

MAIN IDEA: Other organelles have various functions.

Write the function of each organelle. Draw a sketch to help you remember it.

Organelle	Function	Sketch
9. mitochondrion		
10. vacuole		
11. lysosome		
12. centriole		

MAIN IDEA: Plant cells have cell walls and chloroplasts.

13. What role do cell walls play in a plant?

_____

14. What is the difference between a cell wall and a cell membrane?

_____

15. Why are chloroplasts important?

_____

Vocabulary Check

16. Which cell part is a maze of folded membranes where proteins and lipids are produced?

_____

17. Which cell part converts food into energy that is usable by a cell?

_____

SECTION 3.3 | CELL MEMBRANE

Study Guide

KEY CONCEPT

The cell membrane is a barrier that separates a cell from the external environment.

VOCABULARY	
cell membrane	selective permeability
phospholipid	receptor
fluid mosaic model	

MAIN IDEA: Cell membranes are composed of two phospholipid layers.

1. Draw a phospholipid in the box below. Label the three major parts.

2. Which part of a phospholipid is charged, or polar? _____

3. Which part of a phospholipid is nonpolar? _____

4. What type of molecules interact with water, polar or nonpolar? _____

5. Where does a cell membrane come into contact with water? _____

6. Why do the phospholipids surrounding the cell form a bilayer? _____

A cell membrane has other types of molecules embedded in the phospholipid bilayer. List a function of each type of molecule in the table below.

Molecule	Function
7. Cholesterol	
8. Proteins	
9. Carbohydrates	

Section 3.3 STUDY GUIDE CONTINUED

10. In what way is a membrane fluid?

_____

11. Draw a picture in the box below to represent selective permeability.

outside	inside

MAIN IDEA: Chemical signals are transmitted across the cell membrane.

12. A _____ detects a signal molecule and carries out an action in response.

13. A _____ is a molecule that acts as a signal when it binds to a receptor.

14. A ligand that can cross the cell membrane can bind to an _____ receptor.

15. A ligand that cannot cross the cell membrane can send a message to a cell by binding to

a _____ receptor, which then _____ shape.

Vocabulary Check

16. What is the fluid mosaic model?

_____

17. The cell membrane allows some, but not all, molecules to cross. What term describes this property?

_____

SECTION
3.4 | DIFFUSION AND OSMOSIS
Study Guide

KEY CONCEPT

Materials move across membranes because of concentration differences.

VOCABULARY		
passive transport	osmosis	hypotonic
diffusion	isotonic	facilitated diffusion
concentration gradient	hypertonic	

MAIN IDEA: Diffusion and osmosis are types of passive transport.

1. What is a concentration gradient?

_____

2. What does it mean for a molecule to diffuse down a concentration gradient?

_____

Complete the concept map below about passive transport.

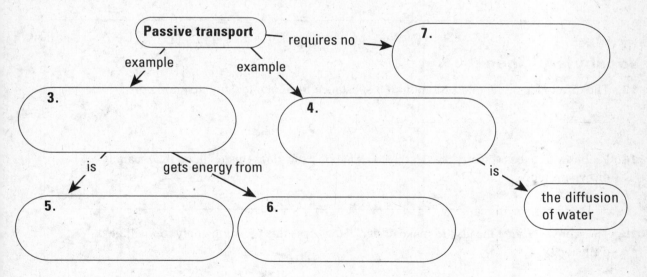

8. The higher the concentration of dissolved particles in a solution, the

_____ the concentration of water molecules in that solution.

Section 3.4 STUDY GUIDE CONTINUED

Suppose you have three solutions with different concentrations of particles. Relative to the concentration of particles in a cell, one solution is isotonic, one is hypertonic, and one is hypotonic. Use this information to answer the next two questions.

9. Which solution has the highest concentration of particles?

_____

10. Which solution has the highest concentration of water molecules?

_____

MAIN IDEA: **Some molecules diffuse through transport proteins.**

11. How does facilitated diffusion differ from simple diffusion?

_____

_____

12. In facilitated diffusion, do molecules move down a concentration gradient or against a concentration gradient?

_____

Vocabulary Check

13. The difference in the concentration of a substance from one location to another is a

_____.

14. People with excess energy are described as hyper. How does this relate to the meaning of hypertonic?

_____

15. The word *facilitate* means "to make easier." How does this meaning apply to facilitated diffusion?

_____

SECTION 3.5

ACTIVE TRANSPORT, ENDOCYTOSIS, AND EXOCYTOSIS

Study Guide

KEY CONCEPT

Cells use energy to transport materials that cannot diffuse across a membrane.

VOCABULARY	
active transport	phagocytosis
endocytosis	exocytosis

MAIN IDEA: Proteins can transport materials against a concentration gradient.

1. How is active transport different than simple diffusion and facilitated diffusion?

   _____

2. How is active transport similar to facilitated diffusion?

   _____

3. List two characteristics that almost all transport proteins share.

   _____

   _____

4. List the key distinguishing feature of active transport proteins.

   _____

5. Refer to Figure 3.25 to draw a picture in the box below to represent active transport.

outside   inside

6. Most active transport proteins use energy from the breakdown of _____ .

CHAPTER 3
Cell Structure and Function

Section 3.5 STUDY GUIDE CONTINUED

MAIN IDEA: Endocytosis and exocytosis transport materials across the membrane in vesicles.

7. A cell may transport a substance in _____ if the substance is

too large to cross the membrane.

8. During endocytosis, the vesicle membrane fuses with a lysosome, and the membrane

and its contents are broken down by _____ .

Complete the Y diagram below to compare and contrast the processes of endocytosis and exocytosis. Under the heading "endocytosis," list the characteristics of endocytosis. Under the heading "exocytosis," list the characteristics of exocytosis. At the bottom of the Y, write the characteristics that both processes have in common. Then lightly cross out those characteristics at the top of the Y.

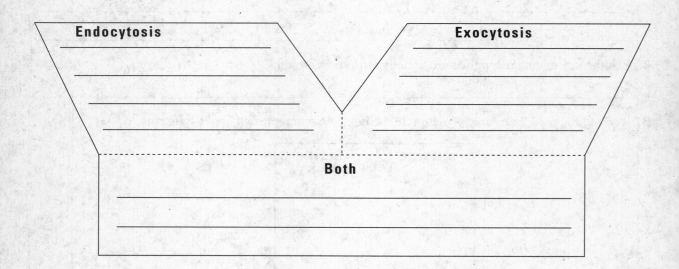

Vocabulary Check

9. What term means "cell eating" and describes a type of endocytosis?

_____

10. The prefix *exo-* means "out of," and the prefix *endo-* means "taking in." How do these meanings relate to the meaning of exocytosis and endocytosis?

_____

_____

11. What process drives molecules across a membrane against a concentration gradient?

_____

SECTION
4.1 | CHEMICAL ENERGY AND ATP
Study Guide

KEY CONCEPT
All cells need chemical energy.

VOCABULARY		
ATP	ADP	chemosynthesis

MAIN IDEA: The chemical energy used for most cell processes is carried by ATP.

1. What do all cells use for energy?

_____

2. What is ATP?

_____

3. What is the relationship between ATP and ADP?

_____

_____

Fill in the four parts of the cycle diagram below to take notes on the relationship between ATP and ADP.

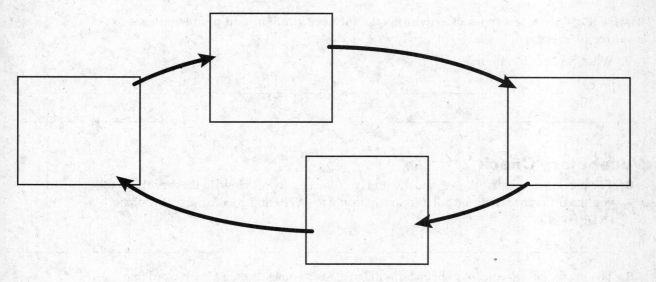

Section 4.1 STUDY GUIDE CONTINUED

MAIN IDEA: **Organisms break down carbon-based molecules to produce ATP.**

Use the table below to organize your notes about the different types of molecules that are broken down to make ATP.

Type of Molecule	Role in ATP Production
Carbohydrates	4.
Lipids	5.
Proteins	6.

MAIN IDEA: **A few types of organisms do not need sunlight and photosynthesis as a source of energy.**

7. What is chemosynthesis?

_____

_____

Vocabulary Check

8. The prefix *tri-* means "three," and the prefix *di-* means "two." How do these prefixes tell you the difference between adenosine triphosphate (ATP) and adenosine diphosphate (ADP)?

_____

9. The prefix *chemo-* means "chemical," and *synthesis* comes from a Greek word that means "to put together." How do these meanings tell you what chemosynthesis does?

_____

_____

OVERVIEW OF PHOTOSYNTHESIS
Study Guide

KEY CONCEPT
The overall process of photosynthesis produces sugars that store chemical energy.

VOCABULARY	
photosynthesis	light-dependent reactions
chlorophyll	light-independent reactions
thylakoid	

MAIN IDEA: Photosynthetic organisms are producers.

1. Why are some organisms called producers?

   _____

2. What is the function of photosynthesis?

   _____

3. What is chlorophyll?

   _____

MAIN IDEA: Photosynthesis in plants occurs in chloroplasts.

4. What are chloroplasts?

   _____

5. In which two parts of a chloroplast does photosynthesis take place?

   _____

6. What are thylakoids?

   _____

7. Write the chemical equation for the overall process of photosynthesis. Then explain what the equation means and identify the reactants, products, and the meaning of the several arrows.

   _____

   _____

   _____

8. What are the differences between the light-dependent reactions and the light-independent reactions?

   _____

   _____

Use the space below to sketch and label a chloroplast. On the sketch, write the four steps of the photosynthesis process.

Photosynthesis

Vocabulary Check

9. The prefix *photo-* means "light," and *synthesis* means "to put together." How do those meanings tell you what happens during photosynthesis?

_____

10. The prefix *chloro-* means "green," and the suffix *-phyll* means "leaf." How are these meanings related to chlorophyll?

_____

11. The prefix *in-* means "not." How does this meaning tell you which reactions in photosynthesis require light, and which reactions do not?

_____

_____

SECTION 4.3

PHOTOSYNTHESIS IN DETAIL

Study Guide

KEY CONCEPT

Photosynthesis requires a series of chemical reactions.

VOCABULARY	
photosystem	ATP synthase
electron transport chain	Calvin cycle

MAIN IDEA: **The first stage of photosynthesis captures and transfers energy.**

1. Overall, what is the function of the light-dependent reactions?

_____

2. What are photosystems?

_____

3. Which molecules carry energy to the light-independent reactions?

_____

Fill in the sequence diagram below to follow the seven steps of the light-dependent reactions.

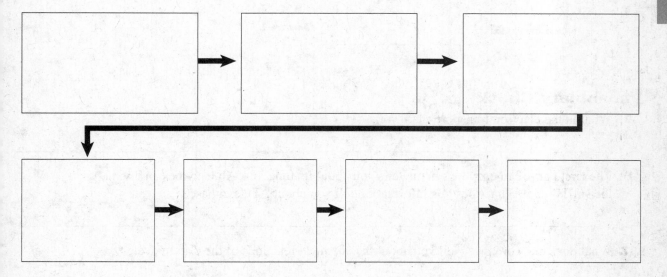

CHAPTER 4
Cells and Energy

Section 4.3 STUDY GUIDE CONTINUED

MAIN IDEA: **The second stage of photosynthesis uses energy from the first stage to make sugars.**

4. What is the function of the Calvin cycle?

_____

Fill in the cycle diagram to summarize the four steps of the Calvin cycle.

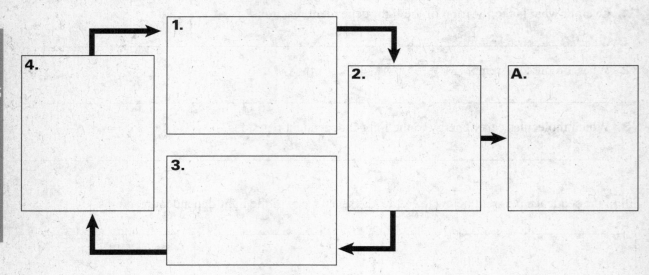

Vocabulary Check

5. What is the electron transport chain?

_____

6. The first part of an enzyme's name tells you about its function. All enzymes end with the suffix -*ase*. What does this information tell you about ATP synthase?

_____

7. What does the word *cycle* tell you about the chemical reactions of the Calvin cycle?

_____

**SECTION
4.4** | OVERVIEW OF CELLULAR RESPIRATION
Study Guide

KEY CONCEPT
The overall process of cellular respiration converts sugar into ATP using oxygen.

VOCABULARY	
cellular respiration	anaerobic
aerobic	Krebs cycle
glycolysis	

MAIN IDEA: Cellular respiration makes ATP by breaking down sugars.

1. What is cellular respiration?

_____

2. Why is cellular respiration called an aerobic process?

_____

3. Where does cellular respiration take place?

_____

4. What happens during glycolysis?

_____

MAIN IDEA: Cellular respiration is like a mirror image of photosynthesis.

5. In what two ways does cellular respiration seem to be the opposite of photosynthesis?

_____

_____

6. In which two parts of a mitochondrion does cellular respiration take place?

_____

7. Write the chemical equation for the overall process of cellular respiration.

_____

8. Explain what the equation means. Identify the reactants, products, and the meaning of the several arrows.

_____

_____

_____

Section 4.4 STUDY GUIDE CONTINUED

Use the space below to sketch and label a mitochondrion. On the sketch, write the four steps of the cellular respiration process that occur in the mitochondrion.

Cellular Respiration

Vocabulary Check

9. The prefix *glyco-* comes from a Greek word that means "sweet." The suffix *-lysis* comes from a Greek word that means "to loosen." How are the meanings of these word parts related to the meaning of *glycolysis*?

_____

_____

10. What does it mean to say that glycolysis is an anaerobic process?

_____

11. What is the Krebs cycle?

_____

_____

SECTION 4.5 | CELLULAR RESPIRATION IN DETAIL
Study Guide

KEY CONCEPT
Cellular respiration is an aerobic process with two main stages.

MAIN IDEA: Glycolysis is needed for cellular respiration.

1. What is the function of glycolysis?

_____

2. What happens to the molecules formed during glycolysis when oxygen is available?

_____

3. What is meant by a "net gain of two ATP molecules" from glycolysis?

_____

MAIN IDEA: The Krebs cycle is the first main part of cellular respiration.

4. What is the function of the Krebs cycle?

_____

Complete the cycle diagram below to summarize the six steps of the Krebs cycle.

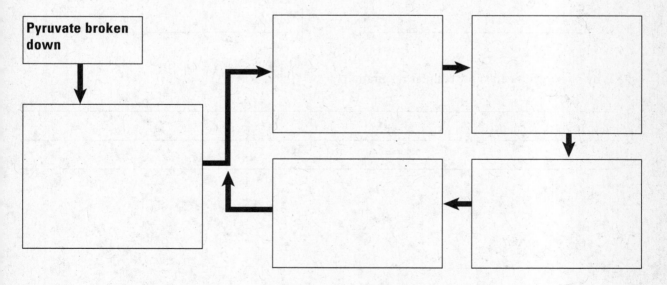

CHAPTER 4
Cells and Energy

Section 4.5 STUDY GUIDE CONTINUED

MAIN IDEA: **The electron transport chain is the second main part of cellular respiration.**

5. Where is the electron transport chain in cellular respiration located?

_____

6. What is the function of the electron transport chain?

_____

Fill in the sequence below to take notes on the four steps of the electron transport chain.

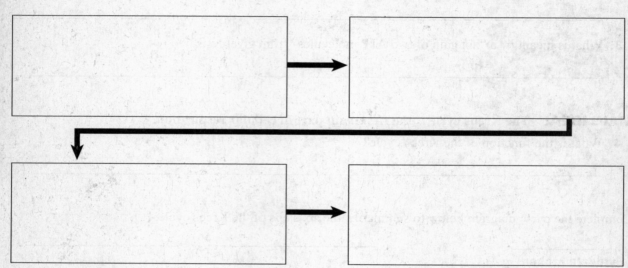

7. Why is oxygen needed for cellular respiration?

_____

_____

_____

CHAPTER 4
Cells and Energy

SECTION
4.6

FERMENTATION
Study Guide

KEY CONCEPT
Fermentation allows the production of a small amount of ATP without oxygen.

VOCABULARY
fermentation
lactic acid

MAIN IDEA: **Fermentation allows glycolysis to continue.**

1. What is the importance of fermentation?

_____

2. What is the function of fermentation?

_____

3. When does fermentation take place in your muscle cells?

_____

4. Why is fermentation an anaerobic process?

_____

5. How is fermentation involved in the production of ATP?

_____

In the space below, show and label the process of lactic acid fermentation.

Lactic Acid Fermentation

CHAPTER 4
Cells and Energy

Section 4.6 STUDY GUIDE CONTINUED

MAIN IDEA: Fermentation and its products are important in several ways.
In the space below, show and label the process of alcoholic fermentation.

Alcoholic Fermentation

6. How are lactic acid fermentation and alcoholic fermentation similar? different?

_____

_____

_____

7. Name one commercial use of lactic acid fermentation.

_____

8. Name one commercial use of alcoholic fermentation.

_____

Vocabulary Check

9. The term *fermentation* is based on a word that means "to bubble." How is this meaning
related to your understanding of the fermentation process?

_____

10. What is lactic acid?

_____

SECTION
5.1

THE CELL CYCLE
Study Guide

KEY CONCEPT
Cells have distinct phases of growth, reproduction, and normal functions.

VOCABULARY

cell cycle   cytokinesis

mitosis

MAIN IDEA: **The cell cycle has four main stages.**

Summarize what happens during each stage of the cell cycle in the boxes below.

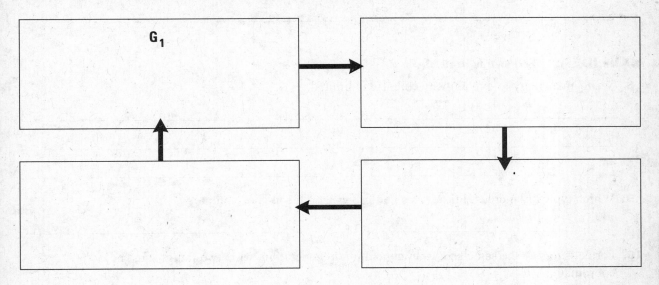

G₁

1. How did the G₁ and G₂ stages get their names?

_____

_____

2. Cells must pass through a critical checkpoint during which two stages of the cell cycle?

_____

3. Where does DNA synthesis happen in eukaryotic cells?

_____

4. What two processes make up the M stage?

_____

MAIN IDEA: Cells divide at different rates.

5. Among different types of cells, which stage of the cell cycle varies most in length?

_____

6. Why does a skin cell divide more often than a liver cell?

_____

7. What is G_0?

_____

MAIN IDEA: Cell size is limited.

8. Write an analogy to explain why cell size is limited.

_____

_____

_____

9. Which typically increases faster as a cell grows, surface area or volume?

_____

10. For cells to stay the same size from generation to generation, what two things must be coordinated?

_____

Vocabulary Check

11. Think of an example of a cycle. What does this cycle have in common with the cell cycle?

_____

_____

12. What process divides a cell's cytoplasm? How do the two word parts of your answer help you remember it?

_____

13. What process divides the cell nucleus and its contents?

_____

SECTION 5.2 | MITOSIS AND CYTOKINESIS
Study Guide

KEY CONCEPT

Cells divide during mitosis and cytokinesis.

VOCABULARY		
chromosome	centromere	metaphase
histone	telomere	anaphase
chromatin	prophase	telophase
chromatid		

MAIN IDEA: Chromosomes condense at the start of mitosis.

1. What is a chromosome?

_____

2. Why do chromosomes condense at the start of mitosis?

_____

3. Why are chromosomes not condensed during all stages of the cell cycle?

_____

_____

Refer to Figure 5.5 to sketch how DNA goes from a long stringy form to a tightly condensed form. Label the parts of the condensed, duplicated chromosome.

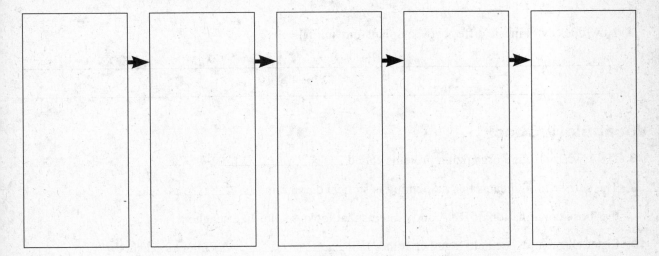

MAIN IDEA: Mitosis and cytokinesis produce two genetically identical daughter cells.

4. How does interphase prepare a cell to divide?

_____

CHAPTER 5
Cell Growth and Division

Section 5.2 STUDY GUIDE CONTINUED

5. Mitosis occurs in what types of cells?

_____

6. Develop a device, such as a short sentence or phrase, to help you remember the order of the steps of mitosis: prophase, metaphase, anaphase, telophase.

_____

Complete the diagram illustrating the four phases of mitosis and one phase of cytokinesis.

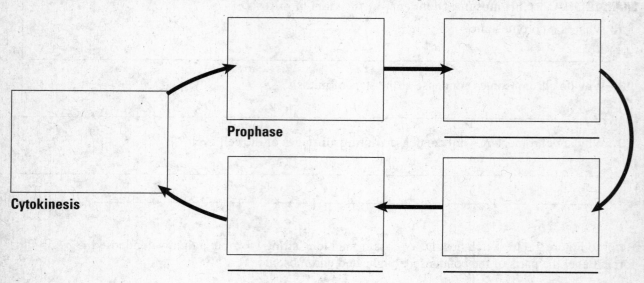

7. How does cytokinesis differ between plant and animal cells?

_____

_____

Vocabulary Check

8. DNA wraps around organizing proteins called _____ .

9. The suffix *-tin* indicates that something is stretched and thin. _____ is

the loose combination of DNA and proteins that looks sort of like spaghetti.

10. Sister chromatids are held together at the _____ , which looks pinched.

11. The ends of DNA molecules form structures called _____ that help

prevent the loss of genes.

SECTION 5.3

REGULATION OF THE CELL CYCLE
Study Guide

KEY CONCEPT

Cell cycle regulation is necessary for
healthy growth.

VOCABULARY		
growth factor	benign	carcinogen
apoptosis	malignant	
cancer	metastasize	

MAIN IDEA: Internal and external factors regulate cell division.

Complete the concept map below to show important ideas about growth factors.

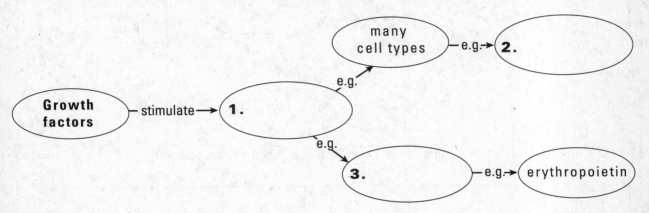

Use the word bank to complete the sequence diagram below.

kinases	cell division	phosphorylate	cyclins

4. _____ →activate→ **5.** _____

6. _____ → target molecules —result in→ **7.** _____

8. What is apoptosis?

_____

MAIN IDEA: Cell division is uncontrolled in cancer.

9. What type of disease may result if cell division is not properly regulated?

_____

CHAPTER 5
Cell Growth and Division

Section 5.3 STUDY GUIDE CONTINUED

Complete the concept map below about cancer cells.

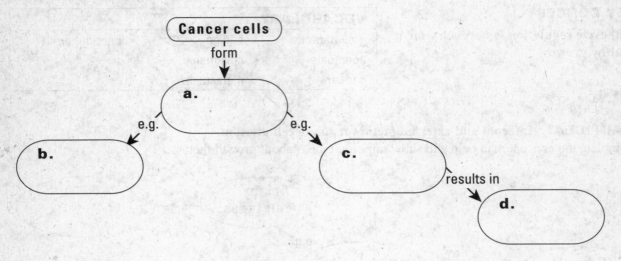

10. List three ways mutations can occur in genes involved in cell-cycle regulation.

_____

Vocabulary Check

11. What does metastasize mean?

_____

12. What is a substance known to produce or promote the development of cancer?

_____

13. Draw a cartoon to help you remember the difference between benign and malignant.

```




```

SECTION 5.4

ASEXUAL REPRODUCTION
Study Guide

KEY CONCEPT
Many organisms reproduce by cell division.

VOCABULARY
asexual reproduction
binary fission

MAIN IDEA: **Binary fission is similar in function to mitosis.**

1. Offspring resulting from asexual reproduction and those resulting from sexual reproduction differ in one major way. What is the difference?

_____

Sketch the steps of binary fission in the boxes below. Beside each sketch, write a brief description of what is occurring.

2. _____

_____

_____

3. _____

_____

_____

4. _____

_____

Section 5.4 STUDY GUIDE CONTINUED

Fill in chart below to highlight the advantages and disadvantages of asexual reproduction.

Advantages	Disadvantages
5.	
6.	
7.	

MAIN IDEA: **Some eukaryotes reproduce through mitosis.**

8. If a eukaryotic organism reproduces through mitosis, what is true about the offspring and the parent organism?

_____

9. In what types of organisms is mitotic reproduction most common?

_____

10. List three examples of mitotic reproduction.

_____

11. What forms of reproduction does the sea anemone use?

_____

Vocabulary Check

12. Write a word that starts with the letters "bi." Explain what is similar between the meaning of the word you wrote and the meaning of "binary fission."

_____

_____

13. What is the creation of offspring from only one parent organism called?

_____

SECTION 5.5

MULTICELLULAR LIFE
Study Guide

KEY CONCEPT
Cells work together to carry out complex functions.

VOCABULARY		
tissue	organ system	stem cell
organ	cell differentiation	

MAIN IDEA: Multicellular organisms depend on interactions among different cell types.

Complete the diagram below that represents organization in multicellular organisms.

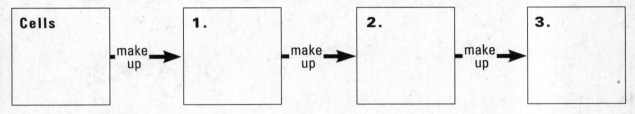

Cells —make up→ **1.** —make up→ **2.** —make up→ **3.**

4. List two examples of tissues found in plants.

_____

5. List two examples of organ systems found in plants.

_____

6. How does an organism benefit from organ systems that work together and communicate?

_____

MAIN IDEA: Specialized cells perform specific functions.

7. What is the process by which unspecialized cells develop into specialized cells?

_____

8. Do different types of cells have different DNA? Explain.

_____

9. What role does cell location play within a developing embryo?

_____

Section 5.5 STUDY GUIDE CONTINUED

MAIN IDEA: Stem cells can develop into different cell types.

Complete the concept map below about stem cell classification.

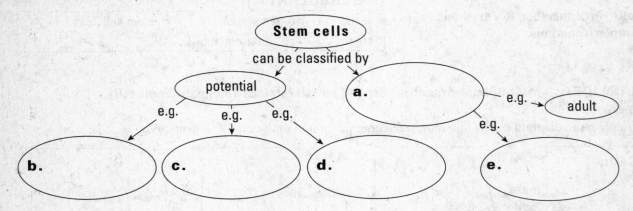

10. List the three identifying characteristics of stem cells.

_____

_____

_____

11. List one advantage of using adult stem cells and one advantage of using embryonic stem cells.

_____

_____

Vocabulary Check

12. What is cell differentiation?

_____

13. Write the following words in order from the largest structure to the smallest structure: cell, organ, organ system, tissue

_____

SECTION 6.1
CHROMOSOMES AND MEIOSIS
Study Guide

KEY CONCEPT

Gametes have half the number of chromosomes that body cells have.

VOCABULARY		
somatic cell	autosome	fertilization
gamete	sex chromosome	diploid
homologous chromosome	sexual reproduction	haploid
		meiosis

MAIN IDEA: You have body cells and gametes.

1. What are the two major groups of cell types in the human body?

_____

2. Where are gametes located?

_____

3. How many chromosomes are in a typical human body cell?

_____

MAIN IDEA: Your cells have autosomes and sex chromosomes.

Fill in the concept map below to summarize what you know about chromosomes.

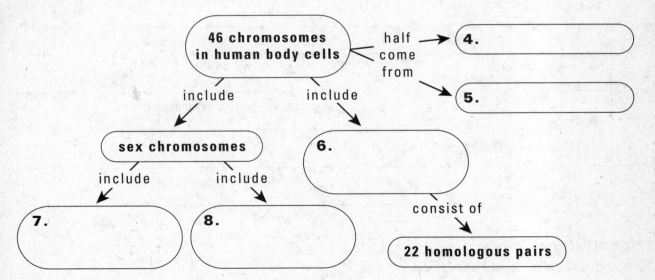

Section 6.1 STUDY GUIDE CONTINUED

CHAPTER 6
Meiosis and Mendel

9. What is the sex of a person with two X chromosomes?

_____

10. Which chromosome carries the fewest number of genes?

_____

MAIN IDEA: **Body cells are diploid; gametes are haploid.**

11. What happens to the nuclei of the egg and sperm during fertilization?

_____

12. What type of cells are haploid?

_____

13. What is the haploid chromosome number in humans?

_____

14. How many autosomes are present in each human gamete? How many sex chromosomes?

_____

15. Complete the following table to summarize the differences between mitosis and meiosis. Use Figure 6.2 to help you.

Mitosis	Meiosis
Makes diploid cells	
	Makes genetically unique cells
Happens throughout lifetime	
	Involved in sexual reproduction

Vocabulary Check

16. What are homologous chromosomes?

_____

17. The word *soma* means "body." How does this relate to the meanings of *autosome* and *somatic cell*?

_____

**SECTION
6.2**

PROCESS OF MEIOSIS
Study Guide

KEY CONCEPT
During meiosis, diploid cells undergo two cell divisions that result in haploid cells.

VOCABULARY	
gametogenesis	egg
sperm	polar body

MAIN IDEA: **Cells go through two rounds of division in meiosis.**

1. After a chromosome is replicated, each half is called a _____ .

2. Two chromosomes that are very similar and carry the same genes are called

_____ .

In the space below, sketch the phases of meiosis I and II and write the name of each phase below it. Use Figure 6.5 to help you.

Meiosis I

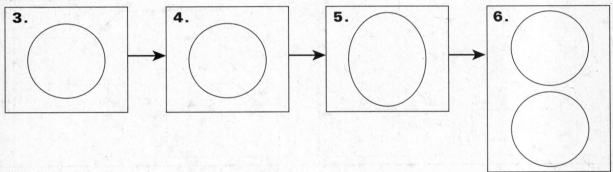

3.

4.

5.

6.

Meiosis II

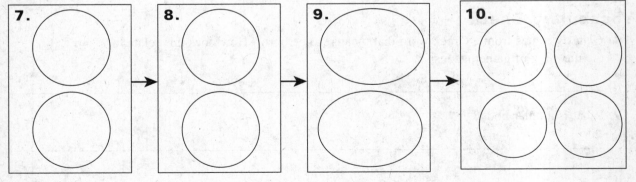

7.

8.

9.

10.

11. During which phase do homologous chromosomes separate?

_____

12. During which phase do sister chromatids separate?

_____

Section 6.2 STUDY GUIDE CONTINUED

MAIN IDEA: **Haploid cells develop into mature gametes.**

13. What does a sperm cell contribute to an embryo?

_____

14. What does an egg contribute to an embryo?

_____

15. Where are polar bodies made, in the male or in the female?

_____

Complete the diagram of gametogenesis in the boxes below. Use Figure 6.6 to help you.

Sperm Formation

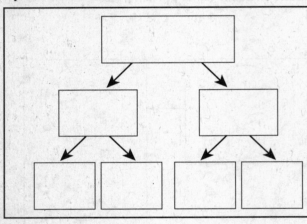

Egg Formation

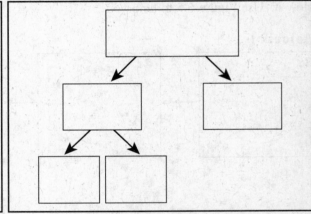

Vocabulary Check

16. *Genesis* comes from a Greek word that means "to be born." How does this relate to the meaning of gametogenesis?

_____

17. What is a polar body?

_____

SECTION 6.3

MENDEL AND HEREDITY
Study Guide

KEY CONCEPT
Mendel's research showed that traits are inherited as discrete units.

VOCABULARY		
trait	purebred	law of segregation
genetics	cross	

MAIN IDEA: Mendel laid the groundwork for genetics.

1. What is genetics?

_____

2. Whose early work is the basis for much of our current understanding of genetics?

_____

3. How did Mendel's views on inheritance differ from the views of many scientists of his time?

_____

_____

MAIN IDEA: Mendel's data revealed patterns of inheritance.

In designing his experiments, Mendel made three important choices that helped him see patterns of inheritance. In the table below, list Mendel's three choices and write an example of how he put each of these choices into action.

Mendel's Choices	Example
4.	
5.	
6.	

7. Why did Mendel use pea plants?

_____

8. Fill in the sequence diagram below to summarize Mendel's experimental process.

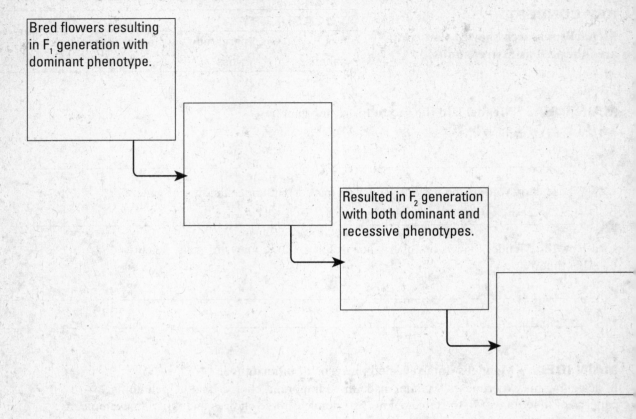

Bred flowers resulting in F_1 generation with dominant phenotype.

Resulted in F_2 generation with both dominant and recessive phenotypes.

9. Mendel concluded that traits are inherited as "discrete units." What do we call these discrete units today?

_____

10. What two conclusions make up Mendel's law of segregation?

_____

_____

Vocabulary Check

11. *Segregation* means "separation." What is "segregated" in Mendel's law of segregation?

_____

12. What does "purebred" mean?

_____

**SECTION
6.4**

TRAITS, GENES, AND ALLELES
Study Guide

KEY CONCEPT
Genes encode proteins that
produce a diverse range of
traits.

VOCABULARY		
gene	heterozygous	phenotype
allele	genome	dominant
homozygous	genotype	recessive

MAIN IDEA: The same gene can have many versions.

1. What is the relationship between a gene and a protein?

_____

2. What is an allele?

_____

3. What term describes a pair of alleles that are the same? that are different?

_____

4. Write a definition of homologous chromosomes using the terms "gene" and "allele."

_____

In the space below, draw a pair of homologous chromosomes. Label the chromosomes with
two sets of genes, one with homozygous alleles (Gene A, Gene A) and one with heterozygous
alleles (Gene B, Gene b).

Section 6.4 STUDY GUIDE CONTINUED

MAIN IDEA: **Genes influence the development of traits.**

5. Write an analogy to show the difference between genotype and phenotype.

_____

_____

6. How are alleles represented on paper?

_____

7. Fill in the table below with the missing genotype, phenotype (dominant or recessive), or alleles (TT, Tt, tt).

Genotype	Phenotype	Alleles
homozygous dominant		
	recessive	
		Tt

8. If an organism has a recessive trait, can you determine its genotype for that trait?

_____

9. What factors besides alleles affect phenotype?

_____

Vocabulary Check

10. What type of alleles are present in an organism with a QQ genotype?

_____

11. What is an alternative form of a gene?

_____

12. What is the opposite of homozygous? of dominant?

_____

SECTION
6.5
TRAITS AND PROBABILITY
Study Guide

KEY CONCEPT
The inheritance of traits follows the rules of probability.

VOCABULARY		
Punnett square	testcross	law of independent assortment
monohybrid cross	dihybrid cross	probability

MAIN IDEA: Punnett squares illustrate genetic crosses.

Identify what each of the numbered parts represents in the Punnett square below. Then draw lines from each of the parents' alleles to the corresponding alleles in the offspring.

2. _____
   _____

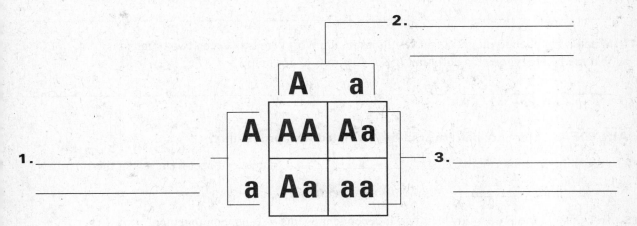

1. _____
   _____

3. _____
   _____

4. Why does each parent contribute only one allele to the offspring?

_____

MAIN IDEA: A monohybrid cross involves one trait.

5. You know a ratio is a comparison that tells how two or more things relate. What is a genotypic ratio? a phenotypic ratio?

_____

_____

6. What is the genotypic ratio of the offspring in Figure 6.15?

_____

7. What is the phenotypic ratio of the offspring in Figure 6.15?

_____

Section 6.5 STUDY GUIDE CONTINUED

MAIN IDEA: **A dihybrid cross involves two traits.**

8. What is a dihybrid cross?

_____

9. Why does each parent organism in the F_1 generation have four alleles listed in Figure 6.17?

_____

10. Suppose an organism had the genotype AABb. What two types of gametes could result from this allele combination?

_____

11. What is the phenotypic ratio that results from a dihybrid cross between two organisms that are heterozygous for both traits? See Figure 6.17 for help.

_____

MAIN IDEA: **Heredity patterns can be calculated with probability.**

12. Probability predicts the _____ number of occurrences, not the

_____ number of occurrences.

13. To calculate the probability that two independent events will happen together,

_____ the probability of each individual event.

14. In Figure 6.18, the probability of getting one coin that is heads up and one coin that is

tails up is _____ .

Vocabulary Check
15. What is a testcross?

_____

16. What is independent in the law of independent assortment?

_____

SECTION 6.6 | MEIOSIS AND GENETIC VARIATION

Study Guide

KEY CONCEPT

Independent assortment and crossing over during meiosis result in genetic diversity.

VOCABULARY

crossing over   genetic linkage

MAIN IDEA: Sexual reproduction creates unique gene combinations.

1. What are two ways that sexual reproduction helps create and maintain genetic diversity?

_____

2. Which does sexual reproduction create, new alleles or new combinations of alleles?

_____

3. How is the production of unique genetic combinations an advantage to organisms and species?

_____

MAIN IDEA: Crossing over during meiosis increases genetic diversity.

4. Are chromosomes in a duplicated or an unduplicated state when crossing over occurs?

_____

Use sketches to illustrate how crossing over contributes to genetic diversity. Use Figure 6.20 for reference. **1.** Draw a cell with four chromosomes in the first box. Make one pair of chromosomes large and the other pair small. Color in one large chromosome and one small chromosome. Leave the other two chromosomes white. **2.** In the next box, draw the cell in prophase I. Have each pair of homologous chromosomes line up together—large with large, small with small. **3.** In the third box, show crossing over between each pair of homologous chromosomes. **4.** In the last box, show what the chromosomes look like as a result of crossing over. You will use this sketch in the next exercise.

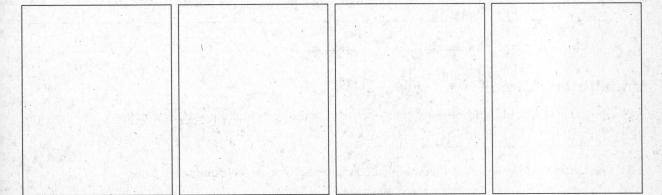

Section 6.6 STUDY GUIDE CONTINUED

Refer to your cell sketch in the last box on the previous page. Also refer to Figure 6.5 if necessary. **1.** In the first box below, show what your cell would look like at the end of meiosis I. Remember, the result will be two cells that have one duplicated chromosome from each homologous pair. **2.** In the second box, show what your cell would look like at the end of meiosis II. Remember, the result will be four cells that have one (*un*duplicated) chromosome from each homologous pair.

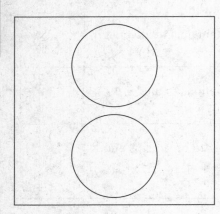 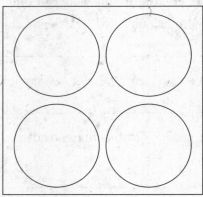

5. If genes A and B are located on separate, nonhomologous chromosomes, will they follow Mendel's law of independent assortment? Explain.

_____

_____

6. If genes A and B are located at opposite ends on the same chromosome, are they likely to follow Mendel's law of independent assortment? Explain.

_____

_____

7. If genes A and B are located very close together on the same chromosome, are they likely to follow Mendel's law of independent assortment? Explain.

_____

_____

Vocabulary Check

8. The exchange of chromosome segments between homologous chromosomes is called

_____ .

9. The tendency for two genes that are located close together on a chromosome to be

inherited together is called _____ .

SECTION 7.1 | CHROMOSOMES AND PHENOTYPE
Study Guide

KEY CONCEPT
The chromosomes on which genes are located can affect the expression of traits.

MAIN IDEA: Two copies of each autosomal gene affect phenotype.

1. What are sex chromosomes?

_____

2. What are autosomes?

_____

3. How is a carrier different from a person who has a genetic disorder?

_____

Complete the two Punnett squares below to compare autosomal recessive disorders with autosomal dominant disorders. Fill in the possible genotypes for offspring, and write in the phenotype (no disorder, carrier, or disorder) for each.

Autosomal Recessive

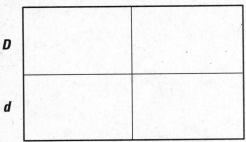

Autosomal Dominant

	D	d
D		
d		

MAIN IDEA: Males and females can differ in sex-linked traits.

4. What are sex-linked genes?

_____

Fill in the Punnett square below to show the pattern of inheritance for sex chromosomes.

Sex Chromosome Inheritance

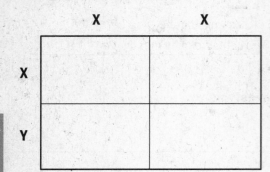

5. In humans, how does a gamete from a male determine the sex of offspring?

_____

6. For what are genes on the Y chromosome responsible?

_____

7. How are sex-linked genes expressed differently in the phenotypes of males and females?

_____

_____

Vocabulary Check

8. The verb *carry* means "to transport." How is the everyday meaning of *carry* related to the meaning of the term *carrier* in genetics?

_____

9. What is X chromosome inactivation?

_____

SECTION 7.2
COMPLEX PATTERNS OF INHERITANCE
Study Guide

KEY CONCEPT

Phenotype is affected by many different factors.

VOCABULARY
incomplete dominance
codominance
polygenic trait

MAIN IDEA: **Phenotype can depend on interactions of alleles.**

1. How is incomplete dominance different from a dominant and recessive relationship?

_____

_____

2. How is codominance different from a dominant and recessive relationship?

_____

_____

3. What is a multiple-allele trait?

_____

_____

In the table below, describe how phenotypes appear in incomplete dominance and codominance. Then sketch an example of each.

Interaction	Phenotype	Example
Incomplete dominance	**4.**	**5.**
Codominance	**6.**	**7.**

Section 7.2 STUDY GUIDE CONTINUED

MAIN IDEA: **Many genes may interact to produce one trait.**
Use the chart below to take notes on polygenic traits and epistasis.

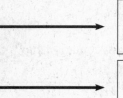

Many genes may interact to produce one trait.

Polygenic Traits

Epistasis

MAIN IDEA: **The environment interacts with genotype.**

8. Why is genotype not the only factor that affects phenotype?

_____

_____

9. List and explain two examples of how environment and genotype can interact.

_____

_____

Vocabulary Check

10. The prefix *in-* means "not." How is the meaning of this prefix related to the meaning of *incomplete dominance*?

_____

11. The prefix *co-* means "together." How is the meaning of this prefix related to the meaning of *codominance*?

_____

12. The prefix *poly-* means "many," and the term *genic* means "related to genes." How do these word parts combine to give the meaning of *polygenic*?

_____

GENE LINKAGE AND MAPPING
Study Guide

KEY CONCEPT
Genes can be mapped to specific locations on chromosomes.

VOCABULARY
linkage map

MAIN IDEA: Gene linkage was explained through fruit flies.

1. What is gene linkage?

_____

2. Why were fruit flies useful in Morgan's research?

_____

3. What is the difference between a wild type and a mutant type?

_____

4. What did Morgan conclude from his research on fruit flies?

_____

_____

Complete the sequence below to take notes about the discovery of gene linkage.

Mendel: Genes assort independently of one another.	→	**Punnett, Bateson:**	→	**Morgan:**

Section 7.3 STUDY GUIDE CONTINUED

MAIN IDEA: **Linkage maps estimate distances between genes.**

5. How is the distance between two genes related to the chance they are inherited together?

_____

6. What hypothesis was the basis of Sturtevant's research?

_____

7. What is a linkage map?

_____

8. How are cross-over frequencies related to linkage maps?

_____

_____

9. What do linkage maps show about genes on a chromosome?

_____

_____

Use the cross-over frequencies given below to draw a linkage map for the four genes listed. Think about the relationship between cross-over frequency and distance in linkage map units. Use Figure 7.11 to help you make the linkage map. Put gene A on the far left of the map, then work through the distances between the gene pairs.

Cross-over Frequencies:	Linkage Map
A-B 20%	
B-C 5%	
A-C 25%	
A-D 7%	
D-B 13%	
D-C 18%	

SECTION 7.4 | HUMAN GENETICS AND PEDIGREES
Study Guide

KEY CONCEPT
A combination of methods is used to study human genetics.

VOCABULARY
pedigree
karyotype

MAIN IDEA: Human genetics follows the patterns seen in other organisms.

1. How does genetic inheritance follow similar patterns in all sexually reproducing organisms?

_____

2. How are single-gene traits useful in studying human genetics?

_____

MAIN IDEA: Females can carry sex-linked genetic disorders.

3. Who can be carriers of autosomal disorders?

_____

4. Why can females, but not males, be carriers of sex-linked genetic disorders?

_____

_____

MAIN IDEA: A pedigree is a chart for tracing genes in a family.

5. What is a pedigree?

_____

6. How are phenotypes used in pedigree analysis?

_____

7. What information on a pedigree can tell you whether a gene is on an autosome or on a sex chromosome?

_____

8. Complete the chart to follow the logic necessary to fill out a pedigree for a sex-linked gene. Use X^D and X^d for the dominant and recessive X-linked genes, respectively.

Tracing Sex-Linked Genes

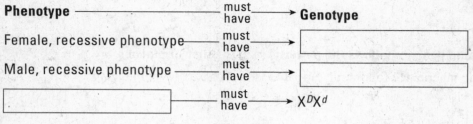

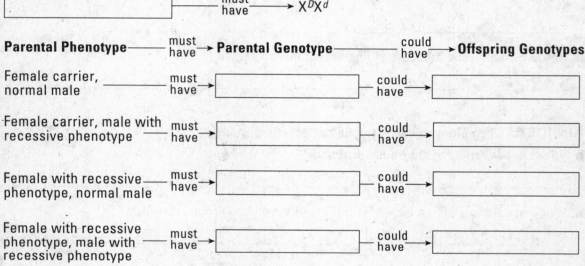

MAIN IDEA: Several methods help map human chromosomes.

9. What are two methods that are used to directly study human chromosomes?

_____

10. What does a karyotype show about chromosomes?

_____

Vocabulary Check

11. What is a karyotype?

_____

SECTION
8.1

IDENTIFYING DNA AS THE GENETIC MATERIAL
Study Guide

KEY CONCEPT
DNA was identified as the genetic material through a series of experiments.

VOCABULARY
bacteriophage

MAIN IDEA: Griffith finds a "transforming principle."
Write the results of Griffith's experiments in the boxes below.

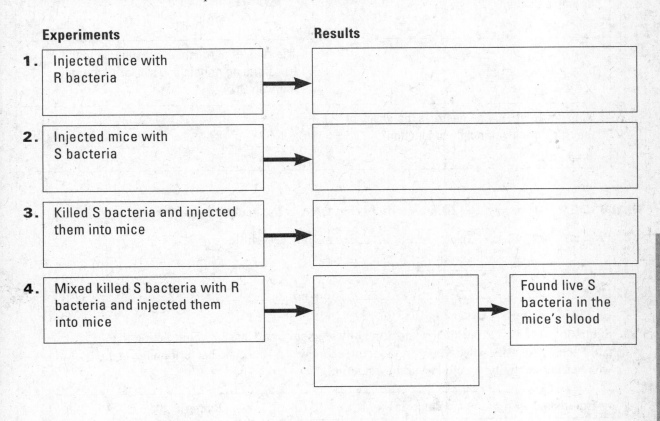

Experiments   **Results**

1. Injected mice with R bacteria

2. Injected mice with S bacteria

3. Killed S bacteria and injected them into mice

4. Mixed killed S bacteria with R bacteria and injected them into mice   Found live S bacteria in the mice's blood

5. Which type of bacteria caused disease, the S form or the R form?

_____

6. What conclusions did Griffith make based on his experimental results?

_____

_____

Section 8.1 STUDY GUIDE CONTINUED

MAIN IDEA: Avery identifies DNA as the transforming principle.

7. Avery and his team isolated Griffith's transforming principle and performed three tests to learn if it was DNA or protein. In the table below, summarize Avery's work by writing the question he was asking or the results of his experiment.

Avery's Question	Results
What type of molecule does the transforming principle contain?	
	The ratio of nitrogen to phosphorus in the transforming principle is similar to the ratio found in DNA.
Which type of enzyme destroys the ability of the transforming principle to function?	

MAIN IDEA: Hershey and Chase confirm that DNA is the genetic material.

8. Proteins contain _____ but very little

_____.

9. DNA contains _____ but no _____.

10. Summarize the two experiments performed by Hershey and Chase by completing the table below. Identify what type of radioactive label was used in the bacteriophage and whether radioactivity was found in the bacteria.

Experiment	Bacteriophage	Bacteria
Experiment 1		
Experiment 2		

Vocabulary Check

11. Explain what a bacteriophage is and describe or sketch its structure.

_____

SECTION
8.2

STRUCTURE OF DNA

Study Guide

KEY CONCEPT
DNA structure is the same in all organisms.

MAIN IDEA: DNA is composed of four types of nucleotides.

In the space below, draw a nucleotide and label its three parts using words and arrows.

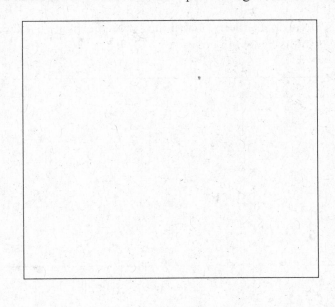

1. How many types of nucleotides are present in DNA?

_____

2. Which parts are the same in all nucleotides? Which part is different?

_____

MAIN IDEA: Watson and Crick developed an accurate model of DNA's three-dimensional structure.

3. What did Franklin's data reveal about the structure of DNA?

_____

4. How did Watson and Crick determine the three-dimensional shape of DNA?

_____

5. How does DNA base pairing result in a molecule that has a uniform width?

_____

MAIN IDEA: **Nucleotides always pair in the same way.**

6. What nucleotide pairs with T? with C?

_____

In the space below, draw a DNA double helix. Label the sugar-phosphate backbone, the nitrogen-containing bases, and the hydrogen bonds.

Vocabulary Check

7. Explain how the DNA double helix is similar to a spiral staircase.

_____

_____

8. How do the base pairing rules relate to Chargaff's rules?

_____

_____

SECTION
8.3

DNA REPLICATION
Study Guide

KEY CONCEPT
DNA replication copies the genetic information of a cell.

<table>
<tr><td>VOCABULARY</td><td></td></tr>
<tr><td>replication</td><td>DNA polymerase</td></tr>
</table>

MAIN IDEA: Replication copies the genetic information.

1. What is DNA replication?

   _____

2. Where does DNA replication take place in a eukaryotic cell?

   _____

3. When is DNA replicated during the cell cycle?

   _____

4. Why does DNA replication need to occur?

   _____

5. What is a template?

   _____

6. If one strand of DNA had the sequence TAGGTAC, what would be the sequence of
   the complementary DNA strand?

   _____

MAIN IDEA: Proteins carry out the process of replication.

7. What roles do proteins play in DNA replication?

   _____

8. What must be broken for the DNA strand to separate?

   _____

9. Why is DNA replication called semiconservative?

   _____

Section 8.3 STUDY GUIDE CONTINUED

Use words and diagrams to summarize the steps of replication, in order, in the boxes below.

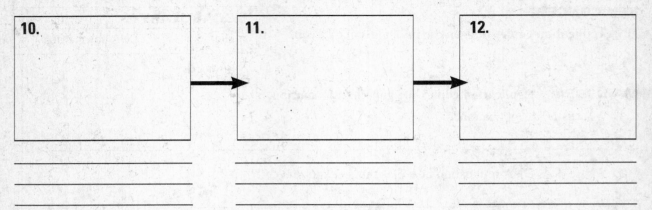

10.   **11.**   **12.**

_____ _____ _____
_____ _____ _____
_____ _____ _____

MAIN IDEA: **Replication is fast and accurate.**

13. Human chromosomes have hundreds of _____ , where the DNA is

unzipped so replication can begin.

14. DNA polymerase has a _____ function that enables it to detect errors

and correct them.

Vocabulary Check

15. Explain what DNA polymerase is by breaking the word into its parts.

_____

16. Write a short analogy to explain what replication is.

_____

Be Creative

17. People sometimes like to display bumper stickers that relate to their trade or field of study. For example, a chemist may have a bumper sticker that says "It takes alkynes to make the world." Then, chemists or other people who know that an alkyne is a molecule that contains carbon atoms joined by a triple bond get a nice little chuckle out of the play on words. Use your knowledge of DNA replication to write a bumper sticker.

_____

_____

SECTION
8.4 | TRANSCRIPTION
Study Guide

KEY CONCEPT

Transcription converts a gene into a single-stranded RNA molecule.

VOCABULARY	
central dogma	messenger RNA (mRNA)
RNA	ribosomal RNA (rRNA)
transcription	transfer RNA (tRNA)
RNA polymerase	

MAIN IDEA: RNA carries DNA's instructions.

Label each of the processes represented by the arrows in the diagram below. Write where each of these processes takes place in a eukaryotic cell in parentheses.

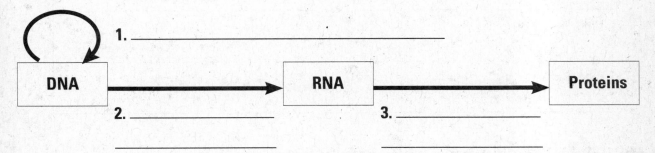

1. _____

2. _____

3. _____

Fill in the table below to contrast DNA and RNA.

DNA	RNA
4. Contains the sugar deoxyribose	
5.	Has the bases A, C, G, and U
6. Typically double-stranded	

MAIN IDEA: Transcription makes three types of RNA.

7. What enzyme helps a cell to make a strand of RNA?

_____

CHAPTER 8
From DNA to Proteins

Section 8.4 STUDY GUIDE CONTINUED

8. Summarize the three key steps of transcription.

_____

_____

_____

9. Write the basic function of each type of RNA in the chart below.

Type of RNA	Function
mRNA	
rRNA	
tRNA	

MAIN IDEA: The transcription process is similar to replication.

10. List two ways that the processes of transcription and replication are similar.

_____

11. List two ways that the end results of transcription and replication differ.

_____

Vocabulary Check

12. How does the name of each type of RNA tell what it does?

_____

_____

13. What is transcription?

_____

SECTION
8.5
TRANSLATION
Study Guide

KEY CONCEPT

Translation converts an mRNA message into a polypeptide, or protein.

VOCABULARY		
translation	stop codon	anticodon
codon	start codon	

MAIN IDEA: **Amino acids are coded by mRNA base sequences.**

1. What is translation?

   _____

2. What is a codon?

   _____

3. Would the codons in Figure 8.13 be found in a strand of DNA or RNA?

   _____

4. What is a reading frame?

   _____

Refer to Figure 8.13 to complete the table below.

Codon	Amino Acid or Function
5. AGA	
6. UAG	
7.	tryptophan (Trp)
8. GGA	

MAIN IDEA: **Amino acids are linked to become a protein.**

9. _____ and _____ are the tools that help a cell translate an mRNA message into a polypeptide.

10. The _____ subunit of a ribosome holds onto the mRNA strand.

11. The _____ subunit of a ribosome has binding sites for tRNA.

12. A tRNA molecule is attached to an _____ at one end and has an

_____ at the other end.

Fill in the cycle diagram below to outline the steps of translation.

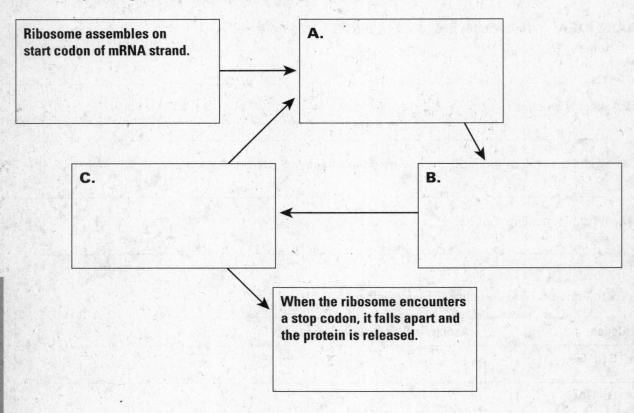

Vocabulary Check

13. What are AGG, GCA, and GUU examples of?

_____

14. What is a set of three nucleotides on a tRNA molecule that is complementary to an mRNA codon?

_____

15. What do codons code for in addition to amino acids?

_____

| GENE EXPRESSION AND REGULATION
Study Guide

KEY CONCEPT
Gene expression is carefully regulated in both prokaryotic and eukaryotic cells.

VOCABULARY	
promoter	exon
operon	intron

MAIN IDEA: Prokaryotic cells turn genes on and off by controlling transcription.

1. Why is gene expression regulated in prokaryotic cells?

_____

2. In prokaryotic cells, gene expression is typically regulated at the start of

_____ .

3. A _____ is a segment of DNA that helps RNA polymerase recognize

the start of a gene.

4. An _____ is a region of DNA that includes a _____ , an

_____ , and one or more _____ that code for proteins

needed to carry out a task.

Complete the cause-and-effect diagram below about the *lac* operon.

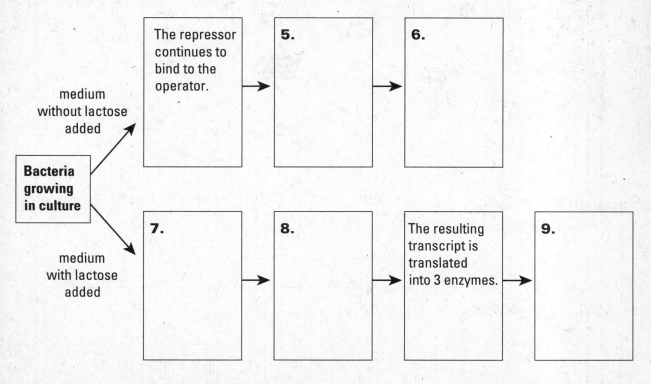

MAIN IDEA: **Eukaryotic cells regulate gene expression at many points.**

10. Why do the cells in your body differ from each other?

_____

11. What role do transcription factors play in a cell?

_____

12. What is a TATA box?

_____

13. What is "sonic hedgehog" an example of?

_____

MAIN IDEA: The diagrams below represent unprocessed and processed mRNA in a eukaryotic cell. Using the diagrams as a reference, fill in the legend with the corresponding element: cap, exon, intron, tail.

Legend

Unprocessed MRNA

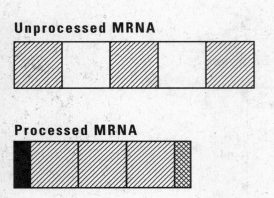

 _____

 _____

Processed MRNA

 _____

 _____

Vocabulary Check

14. What is the difference between an exon and an intron?

_____

_____

15. Make an analogy to help you remember what a promoter is.

_____

SECTION
8.7

MUTATIONS
Study Guide

KEY CONCEPT
Mutations are changes in DNA that may or may not affect phenotype.

VOCABULARY	
mutation	frameshift mutation
point mutation	mutagen

MAIN IDEA: Some mutations affect a single gene, while others affect an entire chromosome.

1. List two types of gene mutations.

_____

2. List two types of chromosomal mutations.

_____

3. Which type of mutation affects more genes, a gene mutation or a chromosomal mutation?

_____

4. What leads to gene duplication?

_____

5. What is a translocation?

_____

Below is a string of nucleotides. **(1)** Use brackets to indicate the reading frame of the nucleotide sequence. **(2)** Copy the nucleotide sequence into the first box and make a point mutation. Circle the mutation. **(3)** Copy the nucleotide sequence into the second box and make a frameshift mutation. Use brackets to indicate how the reading frame would be altered by the mutation.

A G G C G T C C A T G A
6.
7.

CHAPTER 8
From DNA to Proteins

Section 8.7 STUDY GUIDE CONTINUED

MAIN IDEA: **Mutations may or may not affect phenotype.**

Fill in the cause-and-effect diagram below to explain how a point mutation may or may not affect phenotype.

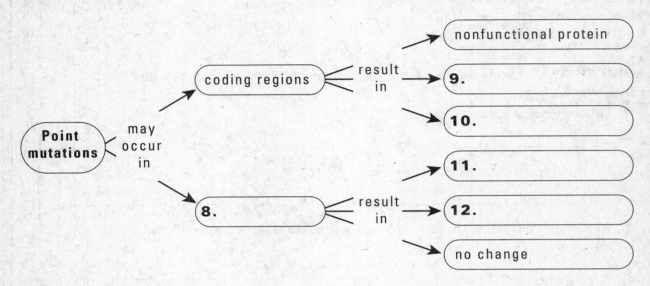

13. For a mutation to be passed to offspring, in what type of cell must it occur?

_____

MAIN IDEA: **Mutations can be caused by several factors.**

14. Can DNA polymerase catch and correct every replication error?

_____

15. What is a mutagen?

_____

16. How does UV light damage the DNA strand?

_____

_____

Vocabulary Check

17. What is a mutation?

_____

18. If a nucleotide is deleted from a strand of DNA, what type of mutation has occurred?

_____

MANIPULATING DNA
Study Guide

KEY CONCEPT
Biotechnology relies on cutting DNA at specific places.

VOCABULARY
restriction enzyme   restriction map
gel electrophoresis

MAIN IDEA: **Scientists use several techniques to manipulate DNA.**

1. List five ways in which scientists study and manipulate DNA.

_____

_____

MAIN IDEA: **Restriction enzymes cut DNA.**

2. What is a restriction enzyme?

_____

3. What is the nucleotide sequence at which a restriction enzyme cuts DNA called?

_____

4. Why would different restriction enzymes cut the same DNA molecule into different numbers of fragments?

_____

In the space provided below, draw two sketches. Show what happens when a restriction enzyme leaves "blunt ends," and show what happens when a restriction enzyme leaves "sticky ends." Label the restriction sites in each sketch.

Blunt Ends	**Sticky Ends**

Section 9.1 STUDY GUIDE CONTINUED

MAIN IDEA: **Restriction maps show the lengths of DNA fragments.**

5. After DNA is cut with a restriction enzyme, how is the mixture of DNA fragments sorted?

_____

6. How does gel electrophoresis work?

_____

_____

_____

_____

7. How do different fragments of DNA show up on a gel?

_____

8. What information does a restriction map give about DNA? What information is not given by a restriction map?

_____

_____

9. How are restriction maps used?

_____

Vocabulary Check

10. How does a restriction enzyme limit, or restrict, the effect of a virus on a bacterial cell?

_____

11. The prefix *electro-* means "electricity." The suffix *-phoresis* comes from a Greek word that means "carrying." How do these two meanings relate to what happens in gel electrophoresis?

_____

SECTION
9.2

COPYING DNA
Study Guide

KEY CONCEPT

The polymerase chain reaction rapidly copies segments of DNA.

VOCABULARY
polymerase chain reaction (PCR)
primer

MAIN IDEA: PCR uses polymerases to copy DNA segments.

1. What is PCR?

_____

2. Why is PCR useful?

_____

MAIN IDEA: PCR is a three-step process.

3. What four materials are needed for PCR?

_____

4. Why are primers needed in the PCR process?

_____

Sketch and label the PCR process in the cycle below.

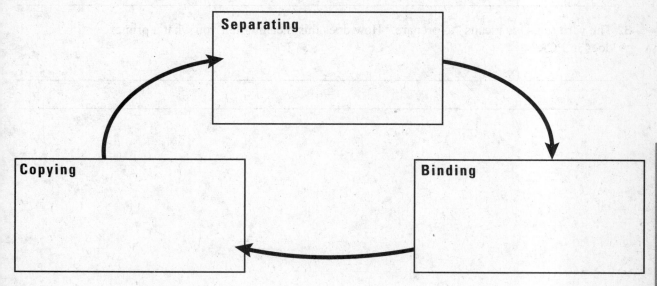

Separating

Copying

Binding

CHAPTER 9
Frontiers of Biotechnology

Section 9.2 STUDY GUIDE CONTINUED

Sketch how the amount of DNA changes during five PCR cycles.

Vocabulary Check

5. DNA polymerase is an enzyme that helps put DNA molecules together. A chain reaction is a process in which one event leads to the next event and the effect is stronger over time. How does the combination of these two terms describe what happens during PCR?

_____

_____

6. The verb *to prime* means "to prepare." How does this meaning tell you what a primer does in PCR?

_____

_____

SECTION
9.3 | DNA FINGERPRINTING
Study Guide

KEY CONCEPT
DNA fingerprints identify people at the molecular level.

VOCABULARY

DNA fingerprint

MAIN IDEA: A DNA fingerprint is a type of restriction map.
Take notes on DNA fingerprinting by filling in the main idea web below.

1. Definition	2. What it shows

DNA fingerprint

3. How it's made	4. What it's based on

5. How is a DNA fingerprint a specific type of restriction map?

_____

_____

MAIN IDEA: DNA fingerprinting is used for identification.

6. How does identification through DNA fingerprinting depend on probability?

_____

_____

_____

7. The chance that two people have four repeats in location A is 1 in 100. The chance that two people have eight repeats in location B is 1 in 50. The probability that two people have three repeats in location C is 1 in 200. What is the probability that two people would have matching DNA fingerprints for these three locations by chance?

_____

_____

8. Why does using more regions of the genome decrease the probability that two people would have the same DNA fingerprint?

_____

_____

9. List two ways in which DNA fingerprinting is used for identification.

_____

_____

Vocabulary Check

10. One definition of the term *fingerprint* is "a distinctive mark or characteristic." How does this meaning relate to a DNA fingerprint?

_____

_____

SECTION
9.4

GENETIC ENGINEERING
Study Guide

KEY CONCEPT

DNA sequences of
organisms can be
changed.

VOCABULARY		
clone	recombinant DNA	transgenic
genetic engineering	plasmid	gene knockout

MAIN IDEA: **Entire organisms can be cloned.**

Fill in the chart below to take notes about cloning.

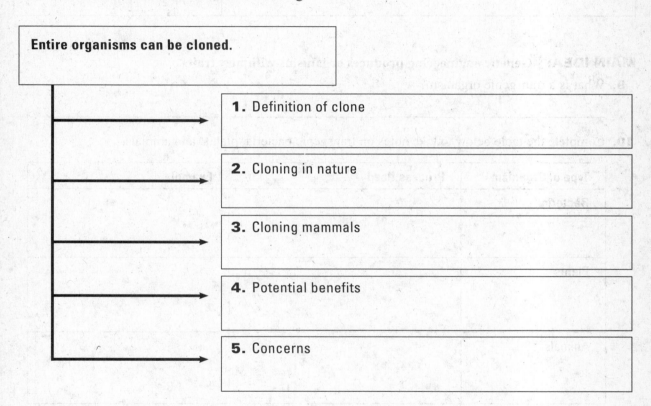

Entire organisms can be cloned.

1. Definition of clone

2. Cloning in nature

3. Cloning mammals

4. Potential benefits

5. Concerns

MAIN IDEA: **New genes can be added to an organism's DNA.**

6. What is genetic engineering?

_____

7. What is recombinant DNA?

_____

8. Why are plasmids used to produce bacteria with recombinant DNA?

_____

Section 9.4 STUDY GUIDE CONTINUED

Use the space below to sketch and label the process that scientists use to produce bacteria with recombinant DNA. Use Figure 9.11 help you with your sketch.

MAIN IDEA: Genetic engineering produces organisms with new traits.

9. What is a transgenic organism?

_____

10. Complete the table below to take notes on transgenic bacteria, plants, and animals.

Type of Organism	Process Used	Example
Bacteria		
Plants		
Animals		

Vocabulary Check

11. The term *recombine* means "to combine, or join, again." How is the meaning of recombine related to the production of recombinant DNA?

_____

12. The prefix *trans-* means "across," and *genic* means "relating to genes." How do these two meanings help to explain the meaning of *transgenic*?

_____

SECTION
9.5 | GENOMICS AND BIOINFORMATICS
          Study Guide

KEY CONCEPT

Entire genomes are
sequenced, studied,
and compared.

VOCABULARY		
genomics	Human Genome Project	DNA microarray
gene sequencing	bioinformatics	proteomics

MAIN IDEA: Genomics involves the study of genes, gene functions, and entire
genomes.

Take notes on concepts in genomics by completing the concept map below.

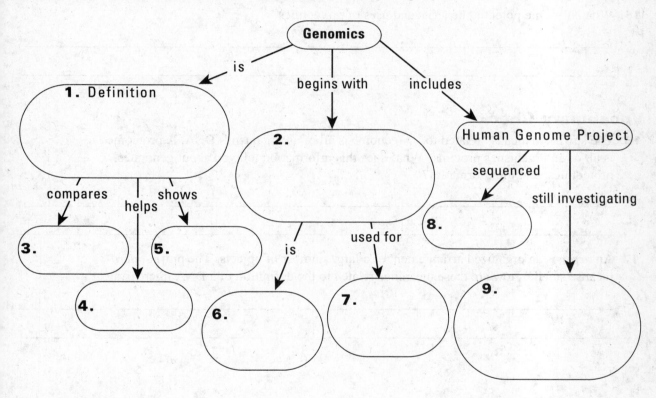

MAIN IDEA: Technology allows the study and comparison of both genes and proteins.

10. What is bioinformatics?

_____

11. Why is bioinformatics important for genomics research?

_____

12. What are DNA microarrays?

_____

Section 9.5 STUDY GUIDE CONTINUED

13. How can DNA microarrays compare gene expression in different cells?

_____

_____

14. What is proteomics?

_____

_____

15. What are some potential benefits and uses of proteomics?

_____

_____

Vocabulary Check

16. The suffix *-ic* means "related to." A genome is all of an organism's DNA. A proteome is all of an organism's proteins. What does this information tell you about genomics, proteomics, and bioinformatics?

_____

_____

17. An *array* is an organized arrangement or a large number of objects. The prefix *micro-* means "small." How are these meanings related to the definition of a DNA microarray.

_____

_____

| GENETIC SCREENING AND GENE THERAPY
Study Guide

KEY CONCEPT
Genetics provides a basis for new medical treatments.

MAIN IDEA: Genetic screening can detect genetic disorders.

1. What is the purpose of genetic screening?

_____

2. How is genetic screening used?

_____

MAIN IDEA: Gene therapy is the replacement of faulty genes.

3. What is the goal of gene therapy?

_____

4. What are two technical challenges in gene therapy?

_____

_____

5. What is one experimental method for the treatment of cancer?

_____

_____

Vocabulary Check

6. The verb *to screen* means "to examine." Explain how this meaning is related to genetic screening.

_____

7. What is gene therapy?

_____

Advertise or Fight Against Genetic Screening

Choose one of the two following situations.

1. Suppose you work for a company that does genetic screening. Draw and write a one-page advertisement that explains genetic screening and what it both can and cannot do.

2. Suppose you are a spokesperson for a group that is against genetic screening. Draw and write a one-page advertisement that focuses on the ethical questions surrounding genetic screening.

SECTION 10.1 | EARLY IDEAS ABOUT EVOLUTION
Study Guide

KEY CONCEPT
There were theories of biological and geologic change before Darwin.

VOCABULARY		
evolution	fossil	gradualism
species	catastrophism	uniformitarianism

MAIN IDEA: **Early scientists proposed ideas about evolution.**

In a phrase, tell what each scientist did to help develop evolutionary theory.

Scientist	Contribution to Evolutionary Theory
1. Linnaeus	
2. Buffon	
3. E. Darwin	
4. Lamarck	

5. What two conditions must be true for a group of animals to be considered the same species?

_____

_____

6. Lamarck's ideas of evolution are known as the inheritance of acquired characteristics. What was incorrect about his theory of how organisms evolve?

_____

_____

7. In the 1700s, many people believed that species were fixed and did not change. How did plant hybridization—a type of crossing that could be observed in experiments—help change this view?

_____

_____

Section 10.1 STUDY GUIDE CONTINUED

MAIN IDEA: Theories of geologic change set the stage for Darwin's theory.

8. Write a description of each theory in the space provided.

Geologic Theory	Description
catastrophism	
gradualism	
uniformitarianism	

Vocabulary Check

9. What word refers to traces of an organism that existed in the past?

_____

10. What is the process of biological change by which descendants come to differ from their ancestors?

_____

11. Events such as volcanoes, floods, and earthquakes are the basis of what geologic theory?

_____

12. What geologic theory can be summarized by the phrase "the present is the key to the past"?

_____

Who's Who

Linnaeus	Lamarck	Buffon	E. Darwin

_____ **13.** Charles Darwin's poetic grandfather

_____ **14.** Thought that a giraffe's long neck evolved from reaching high in trees

_____ **15.** Grouped living organisms into categories based on what they looked like

_____ **16.** Wrote *Historie Naturelle* (Natural History) in 1749

SECTION
10.2 | DARWIN'S OBSERVATIONS
Study Guide

KEY CONCEPT
Darwin's voyage provided insights into evolution.

VOCABULARY
variation
adaptation

MAIN IDEA: Darwin observed differences among island species.

1. What is variation among members of *different* species called?

_____

2. What is variation among members of *the same* species called?

_____

3. What island chain in South America was the source of many of Darwin's insights?

_____

4. Darwin saw populations of various species that seemed well-suited to their environment. What did this suggest?

_____

MAIN IDEA: Darwin observed fossil and geologic evidence supporting an ancient Earth.

5. Darwin observed fossils of huge animals such as *Glyptodon*, a giant armadillo. Why were these fossils of interest to him?

_____

6. Many people in the 1700s thought that Earth was only about 6000 years old. How did the fossil organisms Darwin saw lead him to think Earth must be much older than that?

_____

7. Darwin also observed fossil shells of marine organisms high up in the Andes mountains, and saw an earthquake move land that was underwater move above sea level. How did he apply these insights to the evolution of organisms?

_____

8. Look at Figure 10.4 in your textbook. What differences between the two Galápagos tortoises can you identify from the two pictures?

_____

Section 10.2 STUDY GUIDE CONTINUED

Vocabulary Check

variation	adaptation

_____ **9.** the difference in the physical traits of an individual from those of other individuals in the group to which it belongs

_____ **10.** a feature that allows an organism to better survive in its environment

_____ **11.** A tortoise population lives in an area with high grass. These tortoises have longer necks than tortoises that live in other areas. The long necks are an example of this.

_____ **12.** One bird in a population has a slightly thicker beak than its relatives. This thicker beak is an example of what in the population.

Be Creative

In the space below, draw a sketch of a bird that may eat the food choice that is given in the left column.

Food choice	Sketch
Eats large, hard-shelled nuts	
Eats fruit and insects	

SECTION 10.3 | THEORY OF NATURAL SELECTION
Study Guide

KEY CONCEPT
Darwin proposed natural selection as a mechanism for evolution.

VOCABULARY		
artificial selection	natural selection	fitness
heritability	population	

MAIN IDEA: Several key insights led to Darwin's idea for natural selection.

1. Why did artificial selection interest Darwin?

_____

_____

2. Why must selected traits be heritable?

_____

_____

3. In natural selection, what must be true of traits that are passed down through generations?

_____

_____

4. What important idea from Thomas Malthus inspired Darwin?

_____

_____

MAIN IDEA: Natural selection explains how evolution can occur.

variation	overproduction	adaptation	descent with modification

_____ 5. producing many offspring, some of which may not survive

_____ 6. individual differences that may be heritable

_____ 7. a structure well-suited for the environment

_____ 8. a heritable trait becoming common in a population

Section 10.3 STUDY GUIDE CONTINUED

Use an organism of your choice to sketch the four principles of natural selection.

9. overproduction	**10.** variation
11. adaptation	**12.** descent with modification

MAIN IDEA: Natural selection works on existing variation.

13. Peter and Rosemary Grant observed natural selection acting on traits within a population

    of finches on the Galápagos Islands. A drought reduced the number of small soft

    seeds but left plenty of large, tough-shelled seeds intact. The next year there was a(n)

    _____ (increase, decrease) in the number of large-beaked hatchlings.

14. After several years, the supply of large seeds went down after an unusually wet period.

    The increase in small, soft seeds brought a(n) _____ (increase, decrease)

    in the number of large-beaked hatchlings the following year.

Vocabulary Check

15. *Humans* are the selective agent in which type of process, artificial selection or natural
    selection?

    _____

16. *The environment* is the selective agent in which type of process, artificial selection or
    natural selection?

    _____

17. What is the measure of the ability to survive and produce more offspring relative to
    other members of the population called?

    _____

18. What is the ability of a trait to be passed down from one generation to the next called?

    _____

19. What are all the individuals of a species that live in an area called?

    _____

SECTION
10.4

EVIDENCE OF EVOLUTION
Study Guide

KEY CONCEPT

Evidence of common ancestry among species comes from many sources.

VOCABULARY

biogeography	analogous structure
homologous structure	vestigial structure

MAIN IDEA: Evidence for evolution in Darwin's time came from several sources.

In the diagram below, give examples of each type of evidence for evolution.

1. Fossils:

2. Geography:

Evidence for evolution in Darwin's time came from several sources.

3. Embryology:

4. Anatomy:

MAIN IDEA: Structural patterns are clues to the history of a species.

5. Vestigial structures seem to lack any useful function, or are at least no longer used for their original purpose. Give three examples of vestigial structures.

_____

_____

6. Many modern whale species have vestigial pelvic and leg bones. What does this suggest about the ancestry of modern whales?

_____

Section 10.4 STUDY GUIDE CONTINUED

Vocabulary Check

homologous structure	analogous structure	vestigial structure

_____ **7.** Feature that is similar in structure in different organisms but has different functions

_____ **8.** Feature that performs a similar function in different organisms but is not similar in origin

_____ **9.** Is *not* evidence of a common ancestor

_____ **10.** Remnant of an organ or structure that had a function in an early ancestor

_____ **11.** Examples include the wing of a bat and the hand of a human

_____ **12.** Examples include the wing of a bird and the wing of an insect

_____ **13.** Examples include the wing of an ostrich and the appendix of a human

Sketch it Out

Use Figure 10.11 to sketch a skeleton of a human hand next to the whale fin skeleton shown below. Draw lines to match the groups of bones that are homologous for these two structures.

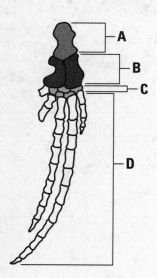

SECTION 10.5

EVOLUTIONARY BIOLOGY TODAY
Study Guide

KEY CONCEPT
New technology is furthering our understanding of evolution.

VOCABULARY
paleontology

MAIN IDEA: **Fossils provide a record of evolution.**

1. What are two reasons that the fossil record is not complete?

_____

2. What is one example of a transitional fossil that has been found?

_____

3. Why are transitional fossils important?

_____

MAIN IDEA: **Molecular and genetic evidence support fossil and anatomical evidence.**

In a phrase, explain how each of the following contribute to evolutionary theory.

Molecular Evidence	Contribution to Evolutionary Theory
4. DNA sequence analysis	
5. Pseudogenes	
6. Homeobox genes	
7. Protein comparisons	

MAIN IDEA: **Evolution unites all fields of biology.**

8. What two things combine to make up our modern evolutionary theory?

_____

_____

9. How has molecular evidence helped support fossil evidence in determining the early ancestor of modern-day whales?

_____

_____

10. What is meant by the phrase "Evolution unites all fields of biology?"

_____

_____

Vocabulary Check

11. How does paleontology contribute to evolutionary biology?

_____

_____

Sketch it Out

Look at the fossil evidence of whale evolution shown in Figure 10.16. Sketch one part of the skeletons (such as the skull, forelimbs, hindlimbs, or ribcages) of each of the whale ancestors. Briefly describe their differences and propose how these differences are well-suited for the habitat in which the animals lived.

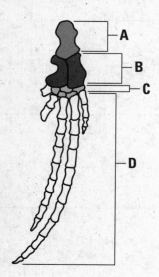

SECTION
11.1

GENETIC VARIATION WITHIN POPULATIONS
Study Guide

KEY CONCEPT
A population shares a common gene pool.

VOCABULARY
gene pool
allele frequency

MAIN IDEA: **Genetic variation in a population increases the chance that some individuals will survive.**

1. What kind of variation must exist in a population that has a wide range of phenotypes?

   _____

2. How can a wide range of phenotypes increase the chance that some individuals will survive in a changing environment?

   _____

   _____

Fill in the concept map below.

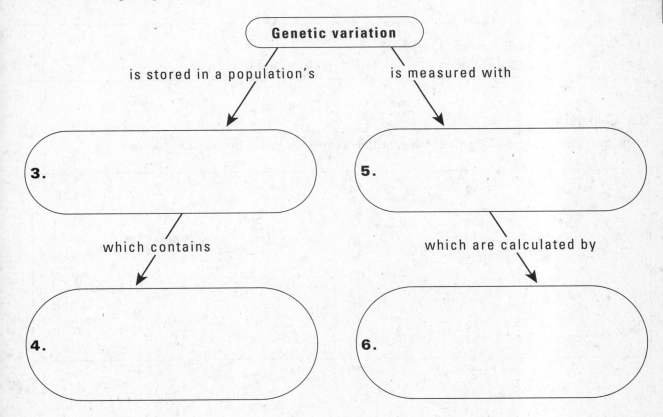

Section 11.1 STUDY GUIDE CONTINUED

MAIN IDEA: Genetic variation comes from several sources.

In a phrase, describe how each term below provides a source of genetic variation.

Source	How It Provides Genetic Variation
7. mutation	
8. recombination	
9. hybridization	

Vocabulary Check

10. How is a gene pool like a pool of genes?

_____

11. What does an allele frequency measure?

_____

Be Creative

In the space below, write a logo advertising the importance of genetic diversity to a population.

SECTION
11.2

NATURAL SELECTION IN POPULATIONS
Study Guide

KEY CONCEPT
Populations, not individuals, evolve.

VOCABULARY	
normal distribution	stabilizing selection
microevolution	disruptive selection
directional selection	

MAIN IDEA: **Natural selection acts on a distribution of traits.**

1. What is a phenotypic distribution?

_____

2. What can you learn from looking at a phenotypic distribution?

_____

_____

3. In a population that is not undergoing natural selection for a certain trait, what does the phenotypic distribution look like?

_____

In the space provided below, draw the phenotypic distribution for a trait that follows a normal distribution. Be sure to label the axes as well as the mean phenotype.

Section 11.2 STUDY GUIDE CONTINUED

MAIN IDEA: Natural selection can change the distribution of a trait in one of three ways.

In the table below, take notes about the three patterns of natural selection.

Type of Selection	How It Works	Graph
4. directional selection		
5. stabilizing selection		
6. disruptive selection		

Vocabulary Check

7. The observable change in _____ over time is called microevolution.

8. During _____ selection, the intermediate phenotype is selected for.

9. During _____ selection, both extreme phenotypes are selected for.

10. During _____ selection, the mean phenotype changes.

OTHER MECHANISMS OF EVOLUTION
Study Guide

KEY CONCEPT

Natural selection is not the only mechanism through which populations evolve.

VOCABULARY		
gene flow	bottleneck effect	sexual selection
genetic drift	founder effect	

MAIN IDEA: **Gene flow is the movement of alleles between populations.**

Fill in the word or phrase that best completes each statement.

1. When an individual _____ from its population, its alleles are

   no longer part of that population's gene pool.

2. When an individual _____ into a new population, the genetic

   diversity of this new population increases.

3. Gene flow among neighboring populations helps to keep the

   _____ of these populations similar.

MAIN IDEA: **Genetic drift can occur in small populations.**

4. How is genetic drift different from natural selection?

   _____

   _____

Use Y-notes to compare and contrast the bottleneck effect and the founder effect.

Bottleneck effect
_____
_____
_____
_____

Founder effect
_____
_____
_____
_____

Both
_____
_____
_____
_____

Section 11.3 STUDY GUIDE CONTINUED

5. Why is genetic drift more likely to occur in smaller populations?

_____

_____

6. What are some problems that can result from genetic drift?

_____

_____

MAIN IDEA: **Sexual selection is a source of evolutionary change.**

7. Why is the cost of reproduction different for males and females?

_____

_____

8. What is sexual selection?

_____

_____

9. _____ selection involves fighting among males for a female,

whereas _____ selection involves males displaying traits

to impress females.

Vocabulary Check

In the spaces provided below, draw pictures that help you to remember the definitions of the vocabulary words.

Gene Flow	Bottleneck Effect	Founder Effect

**SECTION
11.4** | HARDY-WEINBERG EQUILIBRIUM
Study Guide

KEY CONCEPT
Hardy-Weinberg equilibrium provides a framework for
understanding how populations evolve.

VOCABULARY
Hardy-Weinberg equilibrium

MAIN IDEA: Hardy-Weinberg equilibrium describes populations that are not
evolving.

1. What variable remains constant, or in equilibrium, in the Hardy-Weinberg model?

_____

2. Name the five conditions required for a population to be in Hardy-Weinberg equilibrium.

_____

_____

3. Name two ways that population biologists can use Hardy-Weinberg equilibrium.

_____

_____

MAIN IDEA: The Hardy-Weinberg equation is used to predict genotype frequencies
for a population.

4. Write the Hardy-Weinberg equation:

5. Fill in the missing information about the variables involved in the Hardy-Weinberg
equation.

Variable	What It Represents
	frequency of dominant homozygous genotype
2pq	
	frequency of recessive homozygous genotype
p	
	frequency of recessive allele

Section 11.4 STUDY GUIDE CONTINUED

6. In what types of systems can the Hardy-Weinberg equation be used?

_____

7. What variables must be known in order to use the Hardy-Weinberg equation?

_____

8. What can be concluded if real genetic data do not match the frequencies predicted by the equation?

_____

MAIN IDEA: There are five factors that can lead to evolution.

9. Take notes about these five factors in the table below.

Factor	How It Can Lead To Evolution
genetic drift	
gene flow	
mutation	
sexual selection	
natural selection	

Vocabulary Check

10. A population is said to be in Hardy-Weinberg equilibrium for a trait if

_____ stay the same from generation to generation.

SECTION 11.5 | SPECIATION THROUGH ISOLATION
Study Guide

KEY CONCEPT

New species can arise when populations are isolated.

<table>
<tr><td colspan="2">VOCABULARY</td></tr>
<tr><td>reproductive isolation</td><td>geographic isolation</td></tr>
<tr><td>speciation</td><td>temporal isolation</td></tr>
<tr><td>behavioral isolation</td><td></td></tr>
</table>

MAIN IDEA: The isolation of populations can lead to speciation.

Fill in the term from the box that best completes each statement.

speciation	gene flow	species	gene pools
environments	mutation	mate	genetic drift

1. Two populations are said to be isolated if there is no longer any _____ between them.

2. Over generations, the _____ of isolated populations may become more and more different.

3. Isolated populations may become genetically different as they adapt to new _____ , or through random processes such as mutation and _____ .

4. When members of two isolated populations can no longer _____ successfully, the populations are said to be reproductively isolated.

5. Reproductive isolation is the final step of _____ , which is the rise of new _____ .

6. The experiment illustrated in Figure 11.12 shows how just one _____ can provide enough genetic difference to result in reproductive isolation.

Section 11.5 STUDY GUIDE CONTINUED

MAIN IDEA: **Populations can become isolated in several ways.**

7. Name the three types of barriers that can isolate populations.

_____

8. In the chart below, take notes about the three ways in which populations can become isolated, leading to reproductive isolation.

Type of Isolation	How It Works	Example
behavioral isolation		
geographic isolation		
temporal isolation		

Vocabulary Check

9. What is speciation?

_____

10. Which type of isolation involves factors of time?

_____

11. Which type of isolation can involve mating or courtship rituals?

_____

12. Which type of isolation can involve physical barriers?

_____

SECTION 11.6 | PATTERNS IN EVOLUTION
Study Guide

KEY CONCEPT
Evolution occurs in patterns.

VOCABULARY		
convergent evolution	coevolution	punctuated equilibrium
divergent evolution	extinction	adaptive radiation

MAIN IDEA: Evolution through natural selection is not random.

Fill in the Main Idea in the center of the Main Idea Web below. Then take notes based on the phrases in the surrounding boxes.

2. Natural selection has direction:

3. Its effects are cumulative:

1. Main idea:

4. Convergent evolution:

5. Divergent evolution:

MAIN IDEA: Species can shape each other over time.

In the table below, take notes about two ways in which species can coevolve.

Type of Coevolution	How It Works	Example
6. beneficial relationship		
7. evolutionary arms race		

Section 11.6 STUDY GUIDE CONTINUED

MAIN IDEA: Species can become extinct.

In the table below, take notes about background and mass extinctions.

Type of Extinction	Possible Causes	Outcome
8. background extinction		
9. mass extinction		

MAIN IDEA: Speciation often occurs in patterns.

10. The theory of punctuated equilibrium states that relatively brief episodes of

_____ are followed by long periods of little evolutionary

_____ .

11. Adaptive radiation is a process in which one ancestral species diversifies into many

_____ species.

12. Adaptive radiation occurred after the extinction of the dinosaurs, because they left a

wide range of _____ into which mammals could diversify.

Vocabulary Check

13. *Converge* means "to come together" and *diverge* means "to branch out." How do these meanings apply to the terms *convergent* and *divergent evolution*?

_____

_____

14. The prefix *co-* means "together." How does this meaning apply to the term *coevolution*?

_____

15. *Punctuate* means "to interrupt periodically." How does this meaning apply to the term *punctuated equilibrium*?

_____

CHAPTER 11
The Evolution of Populations

THE FOSSIL RECORD
Study Guide

KEY CONCEPT
Fossils are a record of life that existed in the past.

VOCABULARY	
relative dating	isotope
radiometric dating	half-life

MAIN IDEA: Fossils can form in several ways.

In the spaces provided, write either the type of fossil being described or a brief description of how the fossil type is formed.

Type of Fossil	Description of Fossil Formation
1.	Organism trapped in tree resin that hardens after being buried.
2.	An impression is left in sediment, and minerals fill the impression in, recreating the original shape of the organism.
3. Trace fossil	
4. Permineralized fossil	
5.	Organism becomes encased in materials such as ice or volcanic ash, or immersed in a bog.

Section 12.1 STUDY GUIDE CONTINUED

Use Figure 12.2 to fill in a sequence diagram that describes the process of permineralization.

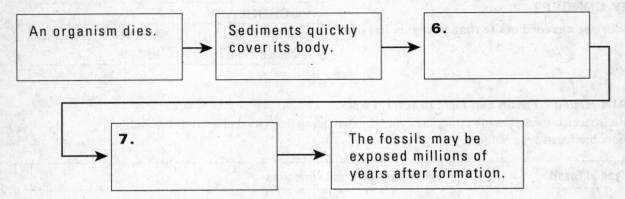

| An organism dies. | → | Sediments quickly cover its body. | → | 6. |

| | 7. | → | The fossils may be exposed millions of years after formation. |

MAIN IDEA: **Radiometric dating provides an accurate estimate of a fossil's age.**

8. What is the main purpose of both relative dating and radiometric dating?

_____

9. What is the main *difference* between relative dating and radiometric dating?

_____

10. How is the radioactive decay of an element used to determine the age of a rock layer?

_____

_____

11. Look at Figure 12.4. After two half-lives, what percentage of carbon-14 remains in a sample?

_____

Vocabulary Check

| relative dating | radiometric dating | isotope | half-life |

_____ **12.** Measures the actual age of a fossil

_____ **13.** Most elements have several of these

_____ **14.** Measure of the release of radiation

_____ **15.** Infers order in which groups of organisms existed

SECTION 12.2

THE GEOLOGIC TIME SCALE
Study Guide

KEY CONCEPT
The geologic time scale divides Earth's history based on major past events.

VOCABULARY		
index fossil	era	epoch
geologic time scale	period	

MAIN IDEA: **Index fossils are another tool to determine the age of rock layers.**

1. How are index fossils used to determine the age of fossils or rock layers?

_____

2. What four characteristics are best for an index fossil to have?

_____

MAIN IDEA: **The geologic time scale organizes Earth's history.**
Look at Figure 12.6 to fill in the following classification tree.

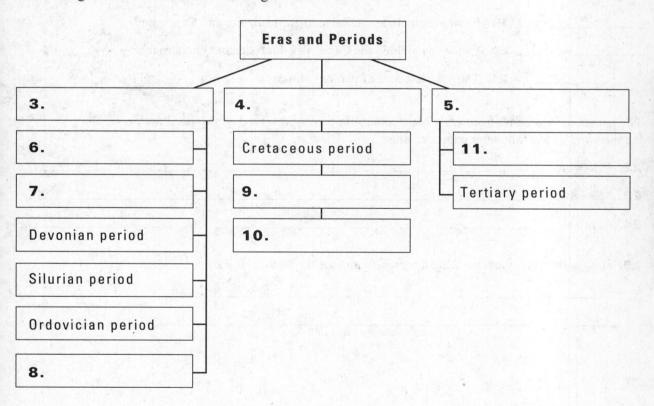

Eras and Periods

- 3.
  - 6.
  - 7.
  - Devonian period
  - Silurian period
  - Ordovician period
  - 8.
- 4.
  - Cretaceous period
  - 9.
  - 10.
- 5.
  - 11.
  - Tertiary period

Vocabulary Check

era	period	epoch

Fill in the blanks below using the terms in the box. You may use some terms more than others.

_____ **12.** The smallest unit of geologic time

_____ **13.** Associated with rock systems

_____ **14.** Consists of two or more periods

_____ **15.** Lasts tens to hundreds of millions of years

_____ **16.** Lasts several million years

_____ **17.** Lasts tens of millions of years

_____ **18.** Most commonly used units of geologic time

_____ **19.** Examples include the Paleozoic, Mesozoic, and Cenozoic

_____ **20.** Examples include the Cambrian, Jurassic, and Quaternary

_____ **21.** The smallest unit of geologic time

The names of eras come from early ideas about life forms preserved as fossils. Provide the meaning of the following names of eras:

22. Paleozoic _____

23. Mesozoic _____

24. Cenozoic _____

25. How is the geologic time scale a representation of the history of Earth?

_____

_____

SECTION
12.3 | ORIGIN OF LIFE
           | # Study Guide

KEY CONCEPT
The origin of life on Earth remains a puzzle.

MAIN IDEA: Earth was very different billions of years ago.

1. Most scientists agree on two points about Earth's origins. What are they?

_____

_____

_____

Fill in the Main Idea Web with the descriptions of early Earth.

Heat released by:

2. _____

and

3. _____

Atmosphere made of:

4. _____

Absent in atmosphere:

5. _____

Earth was very different
billions of years ago.

Eon name:

6. _____

Energy provided by:

7. _____

and

8. _____

Section 12.3 STUDY GUIDE CONTINUED

MAIN IDEA: **Several sets of hypotheses propose how life began on Earth.**
In the column on the left labeled "hypothesis," write the hypothesis from the readings about
how life began on Earth. In the column labeled "proof," list the evidence that supports the
hypothesis. Finally, answer the question at the end of the table.

Hypothesis	Proof
I. ORGANIC MOLECULE HYPOTHESES	
9.	Demonstrated organic compounds could be made by passing electrical current (to simulate lightning) through a closed system that held a mixture of gases (to simulate the early atmosphere).
10. Meteorite hypothesis	
II. EARLY CELL STRUCTURE HYPOTHESES	
11.	Simulated in the lab, making a chimney structure with compartments that could have acted as the first cell membranes.
12. Lipid membrane hypothesis	
III. RNA AS EARLY GENETIC MATERIAL	
13. RNA world hypothesis	

Vocabulary Check

_____ **14.** A cloud of gas and dust in space

_____ **15.** An RNA molecule that can catalyze specific chemical reactions

CHAPTER 12
The History of Life

SECTION 12.4
EARLY SINGLE-CELLED ORGANISMS
Study Guide

KEY CONCEPT
Single-celled organisms existed 3.8 billion years ago.

VOCABULARY

| cyanobacteria | endosymbiosis |

MAIN IDEA: Microbes have changed the physical and chemical composition of Earth.

1. What are two ways that early single-celled organisms changed Earth's surface?

_____

2. What have scientists inferred from fossil stromatolites?

_____

MAIN IDEA: Eukaryotic cells may have evolved through endosymbiosis.
Fill in the blanks with the correct terms.

3. Although prokaryotes existed as long as 3.5 billion years ago, _____ arose

   about 1.5 billion years ago.

4. Eukaryotes have a _____ and membrane-bound organelles.

5. Eukaryotes are _____ , which means they need oxygen to survive.

6. While the first eukaryotes were made of only one _____ , later

   eukaryotes were made of many.

Use the sequence diagram below to summarize the theory of endosymbiosis.

7.		Some of the smaller prokaryotes may have survived.		8.

Section 12.4 STUDY GUIDE CONTINUED

9. Describe the role that cyanobacteria play in the theory of endosymbiosis.

_____

_____

_____

MAIN IDEA: The evolution of sexual reproduction led to increased diversity.

10. What is the main advantage of asexual reproduction?

_____

11. Sexual reproduction increases genetic variation in a population. Why might this be beneficial to the population?

_____

Vocabulary Check

12. Bacteria that can carry out photosynthesis are called _____ .

13. The mutually beneficial relationship in which one organism lives within the body of

another is called _____ .

14. The term *endosymbiosis* can be broken down into parts. *Endo-* means "within." What is another term you have heard that starts with *endo-*?

_____

15. The term *cyanobacteria* can be broken down into parts. *Cyan-* means "greenish blue," because cyanobacteria are often blue-green in color. Not too long ago, cyanobacteria were known as blue-green algae. Why do you think they were considered algae?

_____

KEY CONCEPT
Multicellular life evolved in distinct phases.

VOCABULARY	
Paleozoic	Mesozoic
Cambrian explosion	Cenozoic

MAIN IDEA: **Life moved onto land during the Paleozoic era.**

Fill in a Main Idea and Supporting Information Diagram describing the Paleozoic era.

Life moved onto land during the Paleozoic era.

Early plants moved onto land.

1.

2.

MAIN IDEA: **Reptiles radiated during the Mesozoic era.**

Fill in a Main Idea and Supporting Information Diagram describing the Mesozoic era.

Reptiles radiated during the Mesozoic era.

3.

4.

5.

Section 12.5 STUDY GUIDE CONTINUED

MAIN IDEA: **Mammals radiated during the Cenozoic era.**

Fill in a Main Idea and Supporting Information Diagram describing the Cenozoic era.

Vocabulary Check

Paleozoic	Cambrian explosion	Mesozoic	Cenozoic

_____ **10.** Divided into the Triassic, Jurassic, and Cretaceous periods

_____ **11.** Ended with a mass extinction with more than 90 percent of all marine life extinct

_____ **12.** Earliest part of Paleozoic era

_____ **13.** Primates evolved during this era

_____ **14.** Trilobites were abundant then

_____ **15.** Rise of the first marsupial mammals

_____ **16.** Divided into Tertiary and Quarternary periods

_____ **17.** Life moved onto land

_____ **18.** Includes the Carboniferous period

_____ **19.** Dinosaurs roamed the earth

_____ **20.** Continues today

| PRIMATE EVOLUTION
Study Guide

KEY CONCEPT
Humans appeared late in Earth's history.

VOCABULARY	
primate	hominid
prosimian	bipedal
anthropoid	

MAIN IDEA: Humans share a common ancestor with other primates.
Use Figure 12.18 to help you fill in the concept map below with the correct primate group.

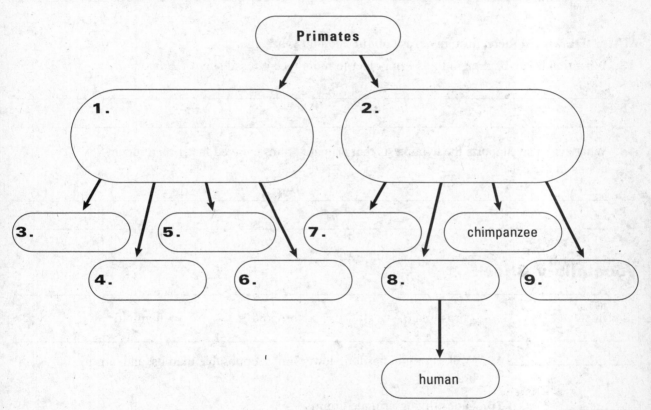

MAIN IDEA: **There are many fossil of extinct hominids.**

10. What are the two groups that most hominid species are classified into?

_____

11. What early hominid was known as "handy man"?

_____

12. What early hominid group may have existed alongside modern humans?

_____

MAIN IDEA: **Modern humans arose about 200,000 years ago.**

13. What trends can be seen in tools from older to more recent fossil sites of *Homo*?

_____

_____

14. What evidence supports the hypothesis that primate brains evolved faster than rodent brains in the past?

_____

_____

Vocabulary Check

primate	prosimian	anthropoid	hominid

_____ **15.** Walks upright, has long lower limbs, opposable thumbs, and large brains

_____ **16.** Oldest living primate group

_____ **17.** Name means humanlike primate

_____ **18.** Has flexible hands and feet, eyes that face forward, and large brains

_____ **19.** Small primate that is active at night

_____ **20.** Includes all species in human lineage, both modern and extinct

_____ **21.** Examples include lemurs, lorises, and tarsiers

_____ **22.** Divided into New World monkeys, Old World monkeys, and hominoids

SECTION 13.1 | ECOLOGISTS STUDY RELATIONSHIPS

Study Guide

KEY CONCEPT
Ecology is the study of the relationships among organisms and their environment.

VOCABULARY	
ecology	ecosystem
community	biome

MAIN IDEA: Ecologists study environments at different levels of organization.
Write a description of each level of organization in the table. Also, provide an example for each level.

Level	Description	Example
1. organism		
2. population		
3. community		
4. ecosystem		
5. biome		

MAIN IDEA: Ecological research methods include observation, experimentation, and modeling.

6. What is observation?

_____

_____

7. What is the difference between direct and indirect surveys?

_____

_____

_____

8. Complete the following table with a benefit and drawback of conducting an experiment in the laboratory compared with conducting an experiment in the field.

Experiment	Benefit	Drawback
Laboratory		
Field		

9. When might a scientist use a model as a research method?

_____

_____

_____

Vocabulary Check

10. What is ecology?

_____

_____

11. Of the three terms, *biome*, *community*, and *ecosystem,* which term contains the other two?

_____

SECTION
13.2

BIOTIC AND ABIOTIC FACTORS
Study Guide

KEY CONCEPT
Every ecosystem includes both living and nonliving factors.

VOCABULARY	
biotic	biodiversity
abiotic	keystone species

MAIN IDEA: **An ecosystem includes both biotic and abiotic factors.**

Use a word from the box below to complete the following sentences.

abiotic	animals	biotic
living	moisture	nonliving
plants	temperature	wind

1. All ecosystems are made up of _____ and

   _____ components.

2. _____ factors are living things, such as

   _____ or _____.

3. _____ factors are nonliving things, such as

   _____, _____, or _____.

MAIN IDEA: **Changing one factor in an ecosystem can affect many other factors.**

4. Describe what biodiversity means in your own words.

   _____

5. What is the term for an organism that has an unusually large effect on its ecosystem?

   _____

6. List a few reasons why a beaver is an example of a keystone species.

   _____

   _____

   _____

Section 13.2 STUDY GUIDE CONTINUED

Vocabulary Check

7. What is the difference between a biotic and an abiotic factor?

_____

_____

8. Take another look at the Visual Vocab on page 403. In architecture, a keystone is the stone at the center of an arch that holds the arch together. How does this definition relate to a keystone species?

_____

_____

Be Creative

In the box below, sketch a simple ecosystem and label the abiotic and biotic factors.

SECTION 13.3 | ENERGY IN ECOSYSTEMS
Study Guide

KEY CONCEPT
Life in an ecosystem requires a source of energy.

VOCABULARY	
producer	heterotroph
autotroph	chemosynthesis
consumer	

MAIN IDEA: Producers provide energy for other organisms in an ecosystem.
Complete the following sentences with the correct term.

autotrophs	eating	nonliving
consumers	heterotrophs	producers

1. _____ are organisms that get their energy from _____

   _____ resources, meaning they make their own food. These

   organisms are also called _____ .

2. _____ are organisms that get their energy by _____ other

   organisms. These organisms are also called _____ .

3. Why are producers so important to an ecosystem?

   _____

   _____

   _____

4. Why is the Sun important to both producers and consumers?

   _____

   _____

   _____

Section 13.3 STUDY GUIDE CONTINUED

MAIN IDEA: Almost all producers obtain energy from sunlight.

5. Complete the following Y-diagram to outline the similarities and differences between photosynthesis and chemosynthesis.

Photosynthesis

Chemosynthesis

_____

_____

_____

_____

_____

_____

Both

_____

_____

_____

Vocabulary Check

6.

Word Part	Meaning
auto-	self
hetero-	other
-troph	nourishment

Use the above word origins to explain the difference between an autotroph and a heterotroph.

_____

_____

7. The prefix *photo-* means "light" while the prefix *chemo-* means "chemical." How do these word origins relate to the difference between photosynthesis and chemosynthesis?

_____

_____

8. What is the difference between a consumer and a producer?

_____

_____

SECTION
13.4 | FOOD CHAINS AND FOOD WEBS
Study Guide

KEY CONCEPT
**Food chains and food webs model the
flow of energy in an ecosystem.**

VOCABULARY	
food chain	decomposer
herbivore	specialist
carnivore	generalist
omnivore	trophic level
detritivore	food web

MAIN IDEA: **A food chain is a model that shows a sequence of feeding relationships.**
Complete the following sentence with the correct terms.

1. A food chain follows the connection between one _____ and a

   single chain of _____ within an _____.

Choose the correct term from the box below to fit each description.

carnivore	herbivore	secondary consumer
decomposer	omnivore	tertiary consumer
detritivore	primary consumer	trophic levels

2. I eat only plants. I am a(n) _____.

3. I eat only other animals. I am a(n) _____.

4. I eat both plants and animals. I am a(n) _____.

5. I eat dead organic matter. I am a(n) _____.

6. I break down organic matter into simpler compounds. I am a(n) _____.

7. I am the first consumer above the producer level. I am a(n) _____.

8. I am a carnivore that eats herbivores. I am a(n) _____.

9. I am a carnivore that eats other carnivores. I am a(n) _____.

10. The levels of nourishment in a food chain are called _____.

CHAPTER 13
Principles of Ecology

MAIN IDEA: **A food web shows a complex network of feeding relationships.**

11. How is a food web different from a food chain?

_____

_____

_____

12. What happens to energy at each link in a food web?

_____

13. What type of organism provides the base of a food web?

_____

_____

_____

Vocabulary Check

14. Use your knowledge of the words *special* and *general* to explain the diets of a specialist and a generalist.

_____

_____

15.

Word Part	Meaning
herba	vegetation
carnus	flesh
omnis	all

Use the word origins to explain the diets of each of the following consumers: herbivores, carnivores, and omnivores.

_____

_____

_____

SECTION
13.5

CYCLING OF MATTER
Study Guide

KEY CONCEPT
Matter cycles in and out of an ecosystem.

VOCABULARY
hydrologic cycle
biogeochemical cycle
nitrogen fixation

MAIN IDEA: Water cycles through the environment.

Fill in the chart with a description of each process that describes how water moves through an ecosystem in the hydrologic cycle.

Process	Description
1. precipitation	
2. evaporation	
3. transpiration	
4. condensation	

MAIN IDEA: Elements essential for life also cycle through ecosystems.

Complete the following sentences with the proper terms.

5. Plants, animals, and most other organisms need _____ for cellular

_____.

6. Oxygen is released as a waste product by plants during the process of

_____. Animals takes in this oxygen and release it as

_____ during the process of _____.

7. In the carbon cycle, plants use energy from the Sun to convert _____

from the air into organic material that becomes a part of the plant's structure.

8. Carbon is released to the atmosphere as carbon dioxide when you breathe during

the process of _____ or through the _____ of dead

organisms.

9. _____, or the burning of fossil fuels, also adds carbon dioxide to the

atmosphere.

10. What is nitrogen fixation?

_____

_____

11. List five steps that occur during the phosphorus cycle.

_____

_____

_____

_____

Vocabulary Check

Use the following word origins to answer the questions below.

Word Part	Meaning
bio-	life
chem-	chemical
geo-	earth
hydro-	water

12. What is a biogeochemical cycle?

_____

_____

13. What is the hydrologic cycle?

_____

_____

SECTION
13.6

PYRAMID MODELS
Study Guide

KEY CONCEPT

Pyramids model the distribution of energy and matter in an ecosystem.

VOCABULARY
biomass
energy pyramid

MAIN IDEA: **An energy pyramid shows the distribution of energy among trophic levels.**

Complete the following sentences with the correct terms.

biomass	heat	waste

1. The measure of the total dry mass of organisms in a given area is called

   _____.

2. When a consumer incorporates the biomass of a producer into its own biomass, a large

   amount of energy is lost as _____ and _____.

3. Label the four tiers of the energy pyramid with the correct trophic level (producers, primary consumers, secondary consumers, tertiary consumers).

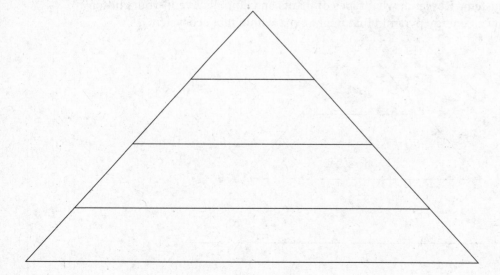

Section 13.6 STUDY GUIDE CONTINUED

CHAPTER 13 Principles of Ecology

MAIN IDEA: Other pyramid models illustrate an ecosystem's biomass and distribution of organisms.

Write a description of each pyramid model.

Model	Description
4. energy pyramid	
5. biomass pyramid	
6. pyramid of numbers	

Vocabulary Check

7. What is biomass?

_____

_____

Make an Energy Pyramid

8. Choose an ecosystem. Research what types of plants and animals live in your chosen ecosystem. Draw an energy pyramid that might exist within that ecosystem.

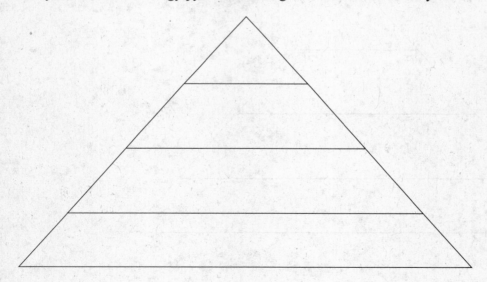

SECTION
14.1

HABITAT AND NICHE
Study Guide

KEY CONCEPT
Every organism has a habitat and a niche.

VOCABULARY	
habitat	competitive exclusion
ecological niche	ecological equivalent

MAIN IDEA: **A habitat differs from a niche.**

1. What is the difference between an organism's habitat and its ecological niche?

_____

_____

2.

food	trees	zebra	grass
hunting behavior	watering hole	sand	savanna
other lions	wildebeest	temperature	

Determine which ecological factors are a part of a lion's niche and which are a part of a lion's habitat by placing the above items in the correct column.

Habitat	Niche

MAIN IDEA: **Resource availability gives structure to a community.**

3. What is competitive exclusion?

_____

_____

4. What are the three possible outcomes of competitive exclusion?

_____

_____

5. What are ecological equivalents?

_____

_____

_____

6. Explain why ecological equivalents do not share the same niche.

_____

_____

_____

Vocabulary Check

7. The term *habitat* comes from a Latin word which means "to dwell." Explain how this word origin relates to the definition of a habitat.

_____

_____

8. In competitive exclusion, who is competing and who gets excluded?

_____

9. What does *equivalent* mean in math? How does that meaning relate to ecological equivalents?

_____

_____

SECTION 14.2

COMMUNITY INTERACTIONS

Study Guide

KEY CONCEPT

Organisms interact as individuals and in populations.

VOCABULARY		
competition	symbiosis	commensalism
predation	mutualism	parasitism

MAIN IDEA: Competition and predation are two important ways in which organisms interact.

Next to each situation described below, write whether it is an example of *inter*specific competition or *intra*specific competition.

_____ **1.** Two squirrels race up a tree to reach a hidden pile of nuts.

_____ **2.** A hyena chases off a vulture to feast on an antelope carcass.

_____ **3.** Different species of shrubs and grasses on the forest floor compete for sunlight.

_____ **4.** Brown bears hunting for fish on a river's edge fight over space.

_____ **5.** Male big horn sheep butt heads violently in competition for mates.

6. Draw and label a sketch that represents an example of a predator-prey interaction.

Section 14.2 STUDY GUIDE CONTINUED

MAIN IDEA: **Symbiosis is a close relationship between species.**

7. For each type of symbiotic relationship, complete the chart with details about how each organism is impacted using the terms "Benefits," "Harmed," or "No impact." For each situation, assume that Organism A initiates the relationship.

Symbiotic Relationship	Organism A	Organism B
mutualism		
commensalism		
parasitism		

8. How is parasitism similar to and different from predation?

_____

_____

9. What is the difference between endoparasites and ectoparasites?

_____

_____

Vocabulary Check

10. The term *symbiosis* comes from a Greek term which means "living together." How does this word origin help to explain the definition of symbiosis?

_____

11. Use your knowledge of the word "mutual" to write a definition for mutualism.

_____

_____

12. The word *commensalism* comes from the Latin *mensa*, meaning "table," and *com-*, meaning "with." If I come to your table to eat your food, I benefit but you don't. Draw a sketch to show this meaning to help you remember it.

SECTION
14.3 | POPULATION DENSITY AND DISTRIBUTION
Study Guide

KEY CONCEPT

Each population has a density, a dispersion, and a reproductive strategy.

VOCABULARY	
population density	survivorship curve
population dispersion	

MAIN IDEA: **Population density is the number of individuals that live in a defined area.**

1. What is the formula for calculating population density?

   _____

2. What might cause the population density of a population of deer to increase?

   _____

MAIN IDEA: **Geographic dispersion of a population shows how individuals in a population are spaced.**

3. In the boxes below, draw and label the three types of population dispersion patterns.

  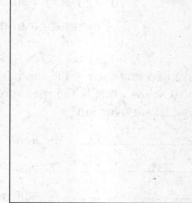

_____   _____   _____

4. List two reasons why a population might live in a clumped dispersion and two reasons why a population might live in a uniform dispersion.

   _____

   _____

CHAPTER 14
Interactions in Ecosystems

MAIN IDEA: **Survivorship curves help to describe the reproductive strategy of a species.**

5. What is meant by the term *reproductive strategy*? What accounts for differences in reproductive strategies?

_____

_____

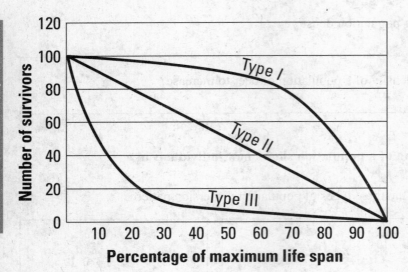

Take a look at each of the survivorship curves shown above. Next to each type of organism listed below, write in the space provided whether it is an example of Type I, Type II, or Type III survivorship.

_____ **6.** lion   _____ **10.** invertebrate

_____ **7.** bird   _____ **11.** fish

_____ **8.** reptile   _____ **12.** giraffe

_____ **9.** small mammal _____ **13.** human

Vocabulary Check

14. What is the difference between population density and population dispersion?

_____

_____

SECTION
14.4 | POPULATION GROWTH PATTERNS
Study Guide

KEY CONCEPT

Populations grow in predictable patterns.

VOCABULARY		
immigration	logistic growth	density-dependent limiting factor
emigration	carrying capacity	density-independent limiting factor
exponential growth	population crash	

MAIN IDEA: Changes in a population's size are determined by immigration, births, emigration, and deaths.

Choose a word from the box below that best completes each sentence.

births	emigration	deaths	immigration

1. When resources are abundant in a particular area, individuals may move into the population of this area. This movement of individuals into a population from a different population is called _____.

2. A very cold winter has left many deer in a population hungry and sick. By the end of the winter, this population will likely decrease because of _____.

3. A deer population experiences growth when the rate of reproduction increases. This change in population size is due to _____.

4. As humans move into their territory, many members of a deer population move away and join other herds. This movement of individuals out of a population into a new population is called _____.

5. How does the availability of resources affect population growth?

_____

_____

Section 14.4 STUDY GUIDE CONTINUED

MAIN IDEA: Population growth is based on available resources.

6. In the space below, draw and label the two different types of population growth curves. Write a brief description next to each graph.

7. What type of population growth curve shows a carrying capacity?

_____

8. What type of population growth is at risk for a population crash? Explain why.

_____

MAIN IDEA: Ecological factors limit population growth.

8. List three examples of density-dependent limiting factors.

_____

9. List three examples of density-independent limiting factors.

_____

Vocabulary Check

Explain why each pair of words below are opposites.

10. emigrate/immigrate

_____

11. density-dependent limiting factor/density-independent limiting factor

_____

12. exponential growth/logistic growth

_____

Name Period Date

SECTION **14.5** | ECOLOGICAL SUCCESSION

Study Guide

KEY CONCEPT

Ecological succession is a process of change in the species that make up a community.

VOCABULARY	
succession	pioneer species
primary succession	secondary succession

MAIN IDEA: Succession occurs following a disturbance in an ecosystem.

1. What is ecological succession?

____

____

2. Fill in the chart below with a description and simple sketch of the four main steps of primary succession. Include the amount of time it takes for each stage of this process.

Section 14.5 STUDY GUIDE CONTINUED

3. Fill in the chart below with a description and simple sketch of the four main steps of secondary succession. Include the amount of time it takes for each stage of this process.

Vocabulary Check

4. What is the difference between primary and secondary succession?

_____

_____

_____

5. Use your knowledge of the word *pioneer* to write a definition for the term *pioneer species*.

_____

_____

_____

LIFE IN THE EARTH SYSTEM
Study Guide

KEY CONCEPT
The biosphere is one of Earth's four interconnected systems.

VOCABULARY		
biosphere	hydrosphere	geosphere
biota	atmosphere	

MAIN IDEA: The biosphere is the portion of Earth that is inhabited by life.

MAIN IDEA: Write a description of each Earth system in the table below.

Earth System	Description
1. biosphere	
2. hydrosphere	
3. atmosphere	
4. geosphere	

5. What is the connection between the biota and the biosphere?

_____

_____

6. Use an example to explain how the four Earth systems are connected.

_____

_____

7. Fill in the following diagram with the correct term (biosphere, biota, hydrosphere, atmosphere, geosphere).

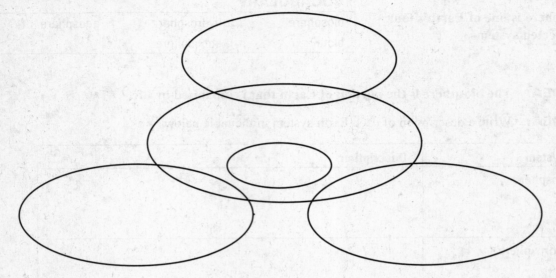

MAIN IDEA: Biotic and abiotic factors interact in the biosphere.

8. In your own words, describe the Gaia hypothesis.

_____

_____

_____

Vocabulary Check

Choose the word from the box below that best matches up with each Earth system.

air	water	earth	life

9. Atmosphere _____

10. Biosphere _____

11. Geosphere _____

12. Hydrosphere _____

SECTION
15.2

CLIMATE
Study Guide

KEY CONCEPT
Climate is a key abiotic factor that affects the biosphere.

VOCABULARY	
climate	microclimate

MAIN IDEA: **Climate is the prevailing weather of a region.**

1. What is the difference between an area's weather and climate?

_____

_____

2. What are four key factors that shape an area's climate?

_____

_____

MAIN IDEA: **Earth has three climate zones.**

3. Name the main reason why the surface of Earth is heated unevenly by the Sun.

_____

_____

4. What characteristic of Earth results in different seasons over a period of a year?

_____

_____

Complete the following chart with the location and characteristics of each climate zone.

Zone	Location	Characteristics
5. polar zone		
6. tropical zone		
7. temperate zone		

CHAPTER 15
The Biosphere

Section 15.2 STUDY GUIDE CONTINUED

8. What effect does the heating of Earth have on air and water movement?

_____

_____

_____

9. Why do areas closer to bodies of water have different climates than do inland areas?

_____

_____

_____

10. How does the presence of mountains affect an area's climate?

_____

_____

_____

_____

11. What is a rain shadow?

_____

_____

Vocabulary Check

12. What is the difference between a climate and a microclimate?

_____

_____

13. List four characteristics of the climate where you live. Include information on temperature and precipitation.

_____

_____

BIOMES

Study Guide

KEY CONCEPT
Biomes are land-based, global communities of
organisms.

VOCABULARY	
canopy	coniferous
grassland	taiga
desert	tundra
deciduous	chaparral

MAIN IDEA: Earth has six major biomes.
Fill in the chart with details about the six major biomes found on Earth.

Biome	Description
1. tropical rain forest	
2. grassland	
3. desert	
4. temperate	
5. taiga	
6. tundra	

7. What is the difference between tropical and temperate grasslands?

_____

_____

8. What are the four different types of deserts?

_____

_____

CHAPTER 15
The Biosphere

Section 15.3 STUDY GUIDE CONTINUED

9. How does precipitation differ in a temperate deciduous forest and a temperate rain forest?

_____

_____

10. Why do few plants grow in the tundra?

_____

_____

11. Describe the main characteristics of chaparral.

_____

_____

MAIN IDEA: Polar ice caps and mountains are not considered biomes.

12. Why aren't polar ice caps and mountains considered biomes?

_____

_____

13. Where are the polar ice caps located?

_____

_____

14. What is a mountain life zone?

_____

_____

Vocabulary Check

15. I lose my leaves in the autumn. I am a _____.

16. I retain my needles all year long. I am a _____.

17. I am the uppermost branches of a tree. I am called the _____.

SECTION 15.4 | MARINE ECOSYSTEMS
Study Guide

KEY CONCEPT
Marine ecosystems are global.

VOCABULARY		
intertidal zone	abyssal zone	phytoplankton
neritic zone	plankton	coral reef
bathyal zone	zooplankton	kelp forest

MAIN IDEA: **The ocean can be divided into zones.**

Complete the following table with information about ocean zones.

Zone	Depth	Description
1. intertidal		
2. neritic		
3. bathyal		
4. abyssal		

5. What zone has the most biomass? What type of organism makes up most of this biomass?

_____

_____

_____

6. Why are phytoplankton critical to life on Earth?

_____

_____

_____

Section 15.4 STUDY GUIDE CONTINUED

MAIN IDEA: Coastal waters contain unique habitats.

7. Complete the following Y-diagram to outline the similarities and differences between a coral reef and a kelp forest.

Coral reef
_____
_____
_____

Kelp forest
_____
_____
_____

Both
_____
_____

8. What is a coral reef made from?

_____

_____

9. Why are coral reefs considered delicate?

_____

_____

Vocabulary Check

10. I am a photosynthetic plankton. What am I? _____

11. I am an animal plankton. What am I? _____

| ESTUARIES AND FRESHWATER ECOSYSTEMS
Study Guide

KEY CONCEPT
Freshwater ecosystems include estuaries
as well as flowing and standing water.

VOCABULARY		
estuary	littoral zone	benthic zone
watershed	limnetic zone	

MAIN IDEA: Estuaries are dynamic environments where rivers flow into the ocean.

1. What is an estuary?

_____

_____

2. What is the distinctive feature of an estuary?

_____

_____

3. Describe why estuaries are considered to be highly productive ecosystems.

_____

_____

4. Why are estuaries sometimes called the "nurseries of the sea"?

_____

_____

5. What adaptations are necessary for organisms that live in an estuary?

_____

_____

6. What impact does the removal of an estuary have on surrounding areas?

_____

_____

CHAPTER 15
The Biosphere

Section 15.5 STUDY GUIDE CONTINUED

MAIN IDEA: **Freshwater ecosystems include moving and standing water.**

7. What are the characteristics of a wetland?

_____

_____

8. What is an important function of wetlands with regard to the water supply?

_____

_____

_____

MAIN IDEA: **Ponds and lakes share common features.**

9. Complete the following chart with details about the different zones found in a pond or lake.

Zone	Location	Description
littoral zone		
limnetic zone		
benthic zone		

Vocabulary Check

10. What is a watershed?

_____

11. The term *estuary* comes from the Latin word *aestus*, which means "tide." How does this meaning relate to the definition of estuary?

_____

_____

HUMAN POPULATION GROWTH AND NATURAL
RESOURCES

Study Guide

KEY CONCEPT

As the human population grows, the demand for Earth's resources increases.

VOCABULARY

nonrenewable resource

renewable resource

ecological footprint

MAIN IDEA: **Earth's human population continues to grow.**

1. Approximately how big is Earth's population now?

_____

_____

2. Name and give examples of two technologies that have influenced human population growth since 1700.

_____

_____

MAIN IDEA: **The growing human population exerts pressure on Earth's natural resources.**

Determine whether the following resources are renewable or nonrenewable. Explain your answer.

3. sun _____

4. oil _____

5. trees _____

6. water _____

7. wind _____

8. corn _____

9. beef _____

10. coal _____

CHAPTER 16
Human Impact on Ecosystems

Section 16.1 STUDY GUIDE CONTINUED

MAIN IDEA: **Effective management of Earth's resources will help meet the needs of the future.**

11. The inhabitants of Easter Island made many mistakes in their resource use. Name one resource that was misused and describe two ways that they could have used the resource more effectively.

_____

12. What is an ecological footprint?

_____

13. List the four factors that determine your ecological footprint.

_____

Vocabulary Check

14. What is the difference between a renewable and a nonrenewable resource?

_____

Be Creative

Create a poster that illustrates why it is important to conserve natural resources.

AIR QUALITY
Study Guide

KEY CONCEPT
Fossil fuel emissions affect the biosphere.

VOCABULARY	
pollution	acid rain
smog	greenhouse effect
particulate	global warming

MAIN IDEA: Pollutants accumulate in the air.

1. What is pollution?

_____

_____

2. What is smog?

_____

_____

3. What are the major components of smog and how does it form?

_____

_____

4. What is acid rain?

_____

_____

5. How does acid rain affect ecosystems?

_____

_____

CHAPTER 16
Human Impact on Ecosystems

Section 16.2 STUDY GUIDE CONTINUED

MAIN IDEA: Air pollution is changing Earth's biosphere.
Complete the concept map with information about the greenhouse effect.

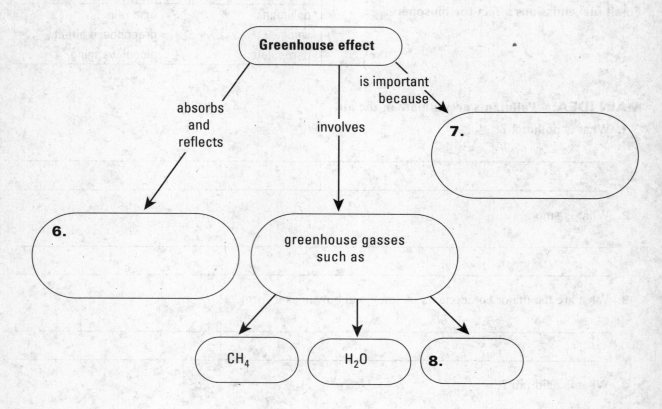

9. What is the greenhouse effect?

_____

10. What is the relationship between the greenhouse effect and global warming?

_____

_____

Vocabulary Check

11. How is a gardener's greenhouse a miniature version of the greenhouse effect?

_____

12. The word *particulate* comes from the Latin word *particula*, which means "a small part."
How is this word origin related to the definition of a particulate?

_____

WATER QUALITY
Study Guide

KEY CONCEPT
Pollution of Earth's freshwater supply threatens habitat and health.

MAIN IDEA: Water pollution affects ecosystems.

1. List three examples of water pollution.

_____

2. Why are indicator species important to scientists?

_____

MAIN IDEA: Biomagnification causes accumulation of toxins in the food chain.

3. What is biomagnification?

_____

_____

4. Illustrate an ecosystem's food chain and describe what will happen to the concentration of pollutants as they move up the food chain.

Section 16.3 STUDY GUIDE CONTINUED

Vocabulary Check

5. Use your knowledge of the prefix *bio-* and the term *magnification* to explain the meaning of biomagnification.

_____

Be Creative

6. Design a poster that explains the importance of keeping sources of fresh water free from pollution.

SECTION 16.4 | THREATS TO BIODIVERSITY
Study Guide

KEY CONCEPT
The impact of a growing human population threatens biodiversity.

MAIN IDEA: Preserving biodiversity is important to the future of the biosphere.

1. What is biodiversity?

_____

_____

2. Why is it important to preserve biodiversity?

_____

_____

3. Where are the highest levels of biodiversity on our planet? Explain why this is so.

_____

_____

MAIN IDEA: Loss of habitat eliminates species.

4. List three ways in which humans cause habitat fragmentation.

_____

_____

MAIN IDEA: Introduced species can disrupt stable relationships in an ecosystem.

5. What is an introduced species?

_____

_____

Section 16.4 STUDY GUIDE CONTINUED

6. Complete the chart below with examples of introduced species and describe how they are disrupting the ecosystem in which they live.

Species	Impact on Ecosystem
Burmese python (Everglades)	
Kudzu (United States)	
Mice (Australia)	

Vocabulary Check

7. A fragment is defined as "a small part broken off or detached." How does this definition relate to the meaning of habitat fragmentation?

_____

_____

Be Creative

8. Think of an area where you live that is an example of habitat fragmentation. Design a poster that both illustrates the problem and proposes a solution.

Name Period Date

SECTION **16.5** | CONSERVATION

Study Guide

KEY CONCEPT

Conservation methods can help protect and restore ecosystems.

VOCABULARY
sustainable development
umbrella species

MAIN IDEA: Sustainable development manages resources for present and future generations.

1. How can sustainable development help Earth's human population?

____

____

2. Complete the following chart with two examples of sustainable development and explain how they benefit humans.

Resource	How Is It managed?	Benefits

MAIN IDEA: Conservation practices focus on a few species but benefit entire ecosystems.

3. What is an umbrella species?

____

____

Section 16.5 STUDY GUIDE CONTINUED

Complete the concept map with information about the manatee and its role as an umbrella species.

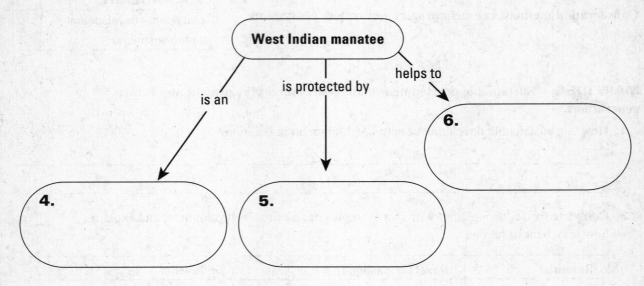

West Indian manatee

is an → **4.**

is protected by → **5.**

helps to → **6.**

MAIN IDEA: **Protecting Earth's resources helps to protect our future.**

7. What are three laws that have been developed to help protect natural resources?

_____

_____

8. What can humans do to reduce their impact on Earth's ecosystems?

_____

_____

Vocabulary Check

9. The word *sustain* means "to keep in existence, maintain." How does this meaning relate to the idea of sustainable development?

_____

_____

SECTION 17.1 | THE LINNAEAN SYSTEM OF CLASSIFICATION
Study Guide

KEY CONCEPT
Organisms can be classified based on physical similarities.

VOCABULARY	
taxonomy	binomial nomenclature
taxon	genus

MAIN IDEA: Linnaeus developed the scientific naming system still used today.

Fill in the concept map with details about Linnaean taxonomy.

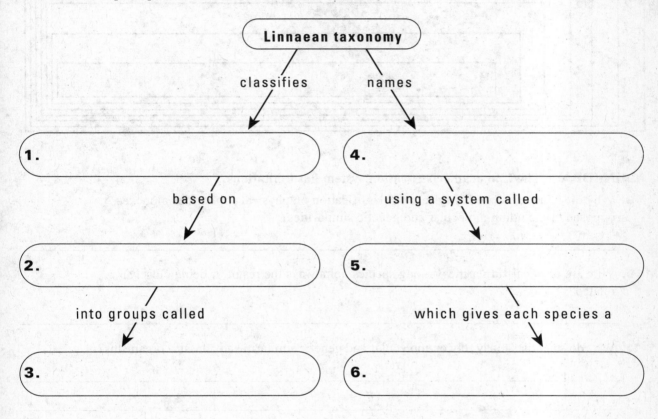

MAIN IDEA: Linnaeus' classification system has seven levels.

7. How are the seven levels of Linnaeus' classification system organized?

_____

8. Describe the trend in the levels, or taxa, as you move down from kingdom to species.

_____

Section 17.1 STUDY GUIDE CONTINUED

Fill in the seven taxa of the Linnaean classification system into the appropriate boxes below.

a.

b.

c.

d.

e.

f.

g.

MAIN IDEA: **The Linnaean classification system has limitations.**

9. Why did Linnaeus base his system of classification on physical similarities alone, as opposed to including molecular and genetic similarities?

_____

10. Why are physical similarities among species not always the result of being closely related?

_____

11. Why do scientists today rely on molecular and genetic similarities to classify organisms?

_____

_____

Vocabulary Check

12. Taxonomy is the science of _____ and _____ organisms.

13. Words from the _____ language are used in binomial nomenclature.

14. In the binomial nomenclature naming system, each species is given a unique scientific

name that includes a _____ name and a _____ descriptor.

SECTION
17.2 | CLASSIFICATION BASED ON EVOLUTIONARY
RELATIONSHIPS
Study Guide

KEY CONCEPT
Modern classification is based on evolutionary relationships.

VOCABULARY	
phylogeny	cladogram
cladistics	derived character

MAIN IDEA: **Cladistics is classification based on common ancestry.**

1. What is a phylogeny?

_____

2. How can a phylogeny be shown?

_____

3. Describe the main goal of cladistics.

_____

Use the word box below to label the main features of a cladogram.

clade	node	taxon being classified	derived character

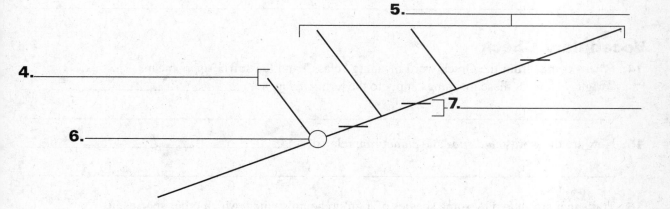

8. What is a clade?

_____

9. How are derived characters used in making a cladogram?

_____

_____

10. On a cladogram, what is a node and what does it represent?

_____

_____

MAIN IDEA: Molecular evidence reveals species' relatedness.

11. Give two examples of molecular evidence that can be used to help determine species'
relatedness.

_____

12. Why are evolutionary trees often changed?

_____

_____

13. What can be concluded if the genes of two species are found to be nearly identical?

_____

Vocabulary Check

14. *Phylo-* comes from the Greek word meaning "class," and the suffix *-geny* means
"origin." How do these meanings apply to the term *phylogeny*? _____

_____

15. How are the words *cladistics* and *cladogram* related? _____

_____

16. Traits that are shared by some species of a group being studied, which other species in

that group do not have, are called _____ characters.

SECTION 17.3 | MOLECULAR CLOCKS
Study Guide

KEY CONCEPT
Molecular clocks provide clues to evolutionary history

VOCABULARY

molecular clock	ribosomal RNA
mitochondrial DNA	

MAIN IDEA: Molecular clocks use mutations to estimate evolutionary time.

1. What are molecular clocks?

   _____

   _____

2. Explain how species become more and more different at the molecular level, after they have diverged from a common ancestor.

   _____

   _____

3. Using Figure 17.8 as a reference, draw your own set of DNA sequences that illustrate molecular evolution.

4. How can scientists estimate mutation rates for use in developing a molecular clock?

   _____

   _____

MAIN IDEA: Mitochondrial DNA and ribosomal RNA provide two types of molecular clocks.

5. Depending on how closely related species are, scientists must choose a molecule with an

   appropriate _____ rate to use as a molecular clock.

6. In the table below, take notes about two commonly used molecular clocks.

Molecular Clock	Description of Molecule	Why It's Unique	How It's Useful as a Molecular Clock
mtDNA			
rRNA			

Vocabulary Check

molecular clock	mitochondrial DNA	ribosomal RNA

_____ **7.** Useful for studying closely related species

_____ **8.** Model that uses mutation rates to measure evolutionary time

_____ **9.** Useful for studying species in different kingdoms or phyla

SECTION 17.4   DOMAINS AND KINGDOMS
Study Guide

KEY CONCEPT
The current tree of life has three domains.

VOCABULARY	
Bacteria	Eukarya
Archaea	

MAIN IDEA: Classification is always a work in progress.

1. Why is classification considered a work in progress?

_____

_____

2. How has the kingdom system changed over the last three hundred years?

_____

_____

3. Describe Woese's discovery and the impact it had on the tree of life.

_____

_____

On the timeline below, fill in the major changes to the kingdom system that have occurred over the past three hundred years.

```
1753:            1938:            1977:



1700        1800        1900        2000
        1866:            1959:
```

Section 17.4 STUDY GUIDE CONTINUED

MAIN IDEA: **The three domains in the tree of life are Bacteria, Archaea, and Eukarya.**

Fill in the table below with notes about the three-domain system.

Domain	Characteristics	Kingdoms Included
4. Bacteria		
5. Archaea		
6. Eukarya		

7. Why is it difficult to classify bacteria and archaea down to the species level?

_____

_____

Vocabulary Check

Bacteria	Archaea	Eukarya

_____ **8.** Have cells with distinct nucleus and membrane-bound organelles

_____ **9.** Known for their ability to live in extreme environments

_____ **10.** Classified by their shape, need for oxygen, and whether they cause disease

SECTION
18.1

STUDYING VIRUSES AND PROKARYOTES
Study Guide

KEY CONCEPT
Infections can be caused in several ways.

VOCABULARY	
virus	viroid
pathogen	prion

MAIN IDEA: Viruses, bacteria, viroids, and prions can all cause infection.

1. In the top left side of the Y shape below, write the characteristics of bacteria.

2. In the top right side of the Y shape below, write the characteristics of viruses.

3. At the bottom of the Y shape below, write the characteristics that both bacteria and viruses share. Then lightly cross out those characteristics at the top of the Y.

Bacteria

_____

_____

_____

_____

Viruses

_____

_____

_____

_____

Both

_____

_____

_____

_____

4. All living things share four characteristics of life. What are they?

_____

_____

Section 18.1 STUDY GUIDE CONTINUED

5. Write the description for each of the infectious particles in the spaces provided on the chart below. Include what they are made of and their range of sizes in your descriptions.

Infectious Particle	Description
Virus	
Viroid	
Prion	

Vocabulary Check

virus	pathogen	viroid	prion

_____ **6.** Does not have genes

_____ **7.** Includes infectious bacteria

_____ **8.** Made of only RNA

_____ **9.** Any living thing or particle that can cause infectious disease

_____ **10.** Made only of protein

_____ **11.** Infects plants

_____ **12.** Made of genetic material surrounded by a protein coat

_____ **13.** Can contain RNA or DNA but is not living

SECTION 18.2 | VIRAL STRUCTURE AND REPRODUCTION
Study Guide

KEY CONCEPT
Viruses exist in a variety of shapes and sizes.

VOCABULARY		
capsid	lytic infection	prophage
bacteriophage	lysogenic infection	

MAIN IDEA: Viruses differ in shape and in ways of entering host cells.

1. Sketch the three common shapes of viruses, and give an example of a virus that exists in each shape.

2. Name the three parts of the structure of a typical enveloped virus.

_____

3. What must viruses do before they can reproduce?

_____

4. How does a virus identify its host?

_____

5. How do the structures of bacteriophages help them infect host cells?

_____

_____

6. What are two ways that viruses that infect eukaryotes enter their host cells?

_____

Section 18.2 STUDY GUIDE CONTINUED

MAIN IDEA: **Viruses cause two types of infections.**

7. In the top left side of the Y shape below, write the characteristics of a lytic infection.

8. In the top right side of the Y shape below, write the characteristics of a lysogenic infection.

9. At the bottom of the Y shape below, write the characteristics that both types of infections have in common. Then lightly cross out those characteristics at the top of the Y.

Lytic infection   **Lysogenic infection**

_____   _____

_____   _____

_____   _____

_____   _____

Both

_____

_____

_____

_____

Vocabulary Check

capsid	bacteriophage	lytic infection	lysogenic infection	prophage

_____ **10.** Virus that infects bacteria

_____ **11.** Viral DNA plus host cell DNA

_____ **12.** Protein shell of a virus

_____ **13.** Infection where virus combines its DNA with host cell's DNA

_____ **14.** Infection where host cell bursts, releasing viral offspring

SECTION
18.3 | VIRAL DISEASES
Study Guide

KEY CONCEPT
Some viral diseases can be prevented with vaccines.

VOCABULARY
epidemic
vaccine
retrovirus

MAIN IDEA: Viruses cause many infectious diseases.

1. What is the body's first defense against infection?

   _____

2. What are two ways viruses enter the body?

   _____

   _____

3. How do some viruses trick cells into letting them in?

   _____

4. Why is it not easy to find a cure for the common cold?

   _____

5. Why must a new flu vaccine be made every year?

   _____

   _____

6. Why might a person who has AIDS have a hard time fighting off normally harmless microorganisms?

   _____

MAIN IDEA: Vaccines are made from weakened pathogens.

7. Describe how a vaccine works to protect people against infection.

   _____

   _____

   _____

Vocabulary Check

epidemic	vaccine	retrovirus

_____ **8.** Contains RNA and uses a special enzyme to make a DNA copy

_____ **9.** Rapid outbreak of an infection that affects many people

_____ **10.** Stimulates the body's own immune response against invading microbes

Identify the Infection

Use Figure 18.10 to determine what infection is being described.

11. Disease caused by the bite of an infected animal

_____

12. Disease caused by the bite of an infected insect

_____

13. Disease caused by contact with a particular rash

_____

14. Disease that causes swelling in glands under a person's jaw

_____

15. Disease that most often infects people in undeveloped countries

_____

CHAPTER 18
Viruses and Prokaryotes

BACTERIA AND ARCHAEA
Study Guide

KEY CONCEPT
Bacteria and archaea are both
single-celled prokaryotes.

VOCABULARY		
obligate anaerobe	plasmid	endospore
obligate aerobe	flagellum	
facultative aerobe	conjugation	

MAIN IDEA: Prokaryotes are widespread on Earth.

1. What two groups of organisms include all prokaryotes on Earth?

_____

2. Some prokaryotes don't need oxygen to live. Where are three environments where
methane-producing archaea have been found?

_____

MAIN IDEA: Bacteria and archaea are structurally similar but have different
molecular characteristics.
In the top left of the Y shape, write the characteristics of bacteria. In the top right, write the
characteristics of archaea. At the bottom, write the characteristics bacteria and archaea have
in common. Then lightly cross out those characteristics at the top of the Y.

Bacteria _____   Archaea _____

_____   _____

_____   _____

_____   _____

Both

_____

_____

_____

_____

Section 18.4 STUDY GUIDE CONTINUED

MAIN IDEA: Bacteria have various strategies for survival.

3. What is binary fission?

_____

4. Describe one way that prokaryotes exchange genetic material.

_____

5. How do some bacteria survive unfavorable conditions?

_____

6. How is an endospore formed?

_____

Vocabulary Check

obligate anaerobe	facultative aerobe	flagellum	endospore
obligate aerobe	plasmid	conjugation	

_____ **7.** Can survive whether oxygen is present or not

_____ **8.** Long whiplike structure used for movement

_____ **9.** Needs oxygen to survive

_____ **10.** Specialized prokaryotic cell that can withstand harsh conditions

_____ **11.** Prokaryotic method of gene exchange

_____ **12.** Cannot live in the presence of oxygen

_____ **13.** Separate circular piece of a prokaryote's genetic material

SECTION
18.5 | BENEFICIAL ROLES OF PROKARYOTES
Study Guide

KEY CONCEPT
Prokaryotes perform important functions for organisms and ecosystems.

VOCABULARY
bioremediation

MAIN IDEA: Prokaryotes provide nutrients to humans and other animals.

1. Some prokaryotes live in animal digestive systems. What are three ways these prokaryotes are helpful to the animals they live inside?

_____

_____

2. What are two ways animals help the prokaryotes that live in their digestive tracts?

_____

3. What are examples of types of food we eat that are fermented by bacteria?

_____

MAIN IDEA: Prokaryotes play important roles in ecosystems.

Write the details about some of the roles prokaryotes play in an ecosystem.

Role	Details
4. Atmosphere composition	
5. Element cycling	
6. Nitrogen fixation	

Section 18.5 STUDY GUIDE CONTINUED

7. Peas, beans, and other legumes have a mutualistic relationship with bacteria. Where do the bacteria associated with these plants live?

_____

_____

8. The bacteria associated with legumes provide nitrogen to the plant in a usable form. Describe how they do this.

_____

_____

9. Some bacteria can digest oil. How are these bacteria helpful?

_____

_____

10. What does the term *biodegradable* mean?

_____

11. What is a type of human-made material that is not biodegradable?

_____

Vocabulary Check

12. The term *bioremediation* can be broken into parts. *Bio-* means "life, or living organism." *Remediation*, or *remedy*, means "the act or process of correcting a fault." How do these word parts relate to what you have learned about bioremediation?

_____

_____

BACTERIAL DISEASES AND ANTIBIOTICS
Study Guide

KEY CONCEPT
Understanding bacteria is necessary to prevent and treat disease.

VOCABULARY
toxin
antibiotic

MAIN IDEA: **Some bacteria cause disease.**

1. What are two ways that bacteria can cause illness?

_____

_____

2. Why are people often unaware of the presence of potentially disease-causing bacteria in their bodies?

_____

3. What are two ways that people can get food poisoning?

_____

MAIN IDEA: **Antibiotics are used to fight bacterial disease.**

4. Why can't antibiotics be used to cure infections caused by viruses?

_____

_____

5. What are two types of organisms that produce antibiotics naturally?

_____

_____

6. What can you do to help prevent getting a bacterial infection?

_____

Section 18.6 STUDY GUIDE CONTINUED

MAIN IDEA: **Bacteria can evolve resistance to antibiotics.**

In the chart below, use your own words to describe the factors that have led to widespread antibiotic resistance.

Factor	Resistance
7. Overuse	
8. Underuse	
9. Misuse	

Vocabulary Check

10. A poison released by a living thing

_____

11. Medicine that helps you fight bacterial infection

_____

Identify the Infection

Use Figure 18.18 to help you identify the infection when given the causes.

12. an open wound that gets dirty

_____

13. breathing in this bacteria's endospores

_____

14. skin making excess oil

_____

15. getting bitten by an infected wood tick

_____

16. many bacteria on teeth and gums

_____

SECTION 19.1

DIVERSITY OF PROTISTS
Study Guide

KEY CONCEPT
Kingdom Protista is the most diverse of all the kingdoms.

VOCABULARY
protist

MAIN IDEA: **Protists can be animal-like, plantlike, or funguslike.**

1. Are protists eukaryotes or prokaryotes?

_____

2. Are all protists single-celled? Explain.

_____

3. Are all protists microscopic? Explain.

_____

4. How do protists reproduce?

_____

Write how each category of protists get their food, and whether they are single-celled, colonial, or multicellular in the table below.

Protist Category	How They Get Their Food	Body Form
Animal-like protist	**5.**	**6.**
7.	**8.**	single-celled, colonial, or multicellular
9.	decomposer (heterotroph)	multicellular

Section 19.1 STUDY GUIDE CONTINUED

MAIN IDEA: Protists are difficult to classify.

10. What kingdom are protists placed in?

_____

11. What domain are protists placed in?

_____

12. Are protists more closely related to animals or to bacteria? Explain.

_____

13. Look at Figure 19.3. What type of protist is more closely related to animals: algae or slime molds?

_____

14. Look again at Figure 19.3. What type of protist is more closely related to plants: algae or slime molds?

_____

Vocabulary Check

15. In the 1860s, the scientist Ernst Haeckel first used the term *Protista* to categorize all single-celled organisms. How has the meaning of *protist* changed since then?

_____

Sketch it Out

Using the six kingdom model of classification shown below, draw two circles. One circle should include all of the prokaryotes. The other circle should include all of the eukaryotes. Be sure to label both of the groups that you have identified.

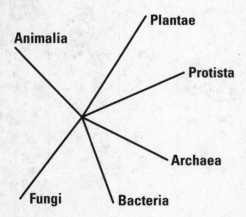

SECTION
19.2 | ANIMAL-LIKE PROTISTS
Study Guide

KEY CONCEPT
Animal-like protists are single-celled heterotrophs that can move.

VOCABULARY	
protozoa	cilia
pseudopod	

MAIN IDEA: Animal-like protists move in various ways.

1. What are protists?

_____

Fill in the table below with characteristics of animal-like protists.

Structure Used for Movement	Way of Life	Example (sketch and label)
Flagella	free-living, parasites, and mutualists	**2.**
3.	free-living, parasites	**4.** amoeba or foraminifera (draw sketch and label)
5.	**6.**	**7.**

CHAPTER 19
Protists and Fungi

Section 19.2 STUDY GUIDE CONTINUED

MAIN IDEA: **Some animal-like protists cause disease.**

8. What is the disease caused by the protist *Plasmodium*?

_____

9. How is the disease caused by *Plasmodium* passed to humans?

_____

10. One protist causes sleeping sickness. What structure does that protist use to move around?

_____

11. What protist is common in natural streams and other bodies of water near wild animal habitats?

_____

Vocabulary Check

12. A common name that refers to all animal-like protists

_____

13. Shorter and more numerous than flagella

_____

14. Means "fake foot"

_____

Sketch it Out

Use Figure 19.5 and the text to sketch and describe how an amoeba gets its food.

PLANTLIKE PROTISTS
Study Guide

KEY CONCEPT
Algae are plantlike protists.

VOCABULARY
algae

MAIN IDEA: Plantlike protists can be single-celled or multicellular.

Fill in the table below with characteristics of plantlike protists.

Plantlike Protist	Where Found	Identifying Characteristic	Single-celled or Multicellular
Euglenoids	fresh water, salt water	1–2 flagella	1.
Dinoflagellates	salt water, fresh water, snow	2.	3.
Diatoms	4.	5.	single-celled
Green algae	6.	chlorophyll a and b, carotenoids	7.
Brown algae	8.	9.	10.
Red algae	11.	chlorophyll a, phycoerythrin	12.

CHAPTER 19
Protists and Fungi

Section 19.3 STUDY GUIDE CONTINUED

MAIN IDEA: Many plantlike protists can reproduce both sexually and asexually.
Choose whether the phrase below best describes asexual reproduction or sexual reproduction of algae.

asexual reproduction	sexual reproduction

_____ **13.** All algae can reproduce this way.

_____ **14.** In *Clamydomonas*, the entire cycle is haploid ($1n$).

_____ **15.** Simple fragmenting.

_____ **16.** In *Clamydomonas*, this is triggered by environmental stress.

_____ **17.** Gametes are formed.

_____ **18.** In *Clamydomonas*, it has both haploid ($1n$) and diploid ($2n$) stages.

Vocabulary Check

19. Are algae plants or protists? Explain.

_____

Sketch it Out

Use Figure 19.15 to sketch the life cycle of a single-celled green algae. Make sure to label asexual and sexual reproduction.

SECTION 19.4 | FUNGUSLIKE PROTISTS
Study Guide

KEY CONCEPT
Funguslike protists decompose organic matter.

<table>
<tr><td>VOCABULARY</td></tr>
<tr><td>slime mold   water mold</td></tr>
</table>

MAIN IDEA: **Slime molds and water molds are funguslike protists.**

1. How are funguslike protists different from fungi?

_____

2. What are the two types of slime molds?

_____

_____

3. The protist that causes malaria is called *Plasmodium*. How is a funguslike protist plasmodium different than this disease-causing *Plasmodium*?

_____

_____

4. What happens to a plasmodial slime mold when it is under environmental stress?

_____

5. What is unusual about the spores released by a slime mold?

_____

_____

6. A cellular slime mold produces a pseudoplasmodium, which means "fake plasmodium." How is a pseudoplasmodium of a cellular slime mold different from a plasmodium of a plasmodial slime mold?

_____

7. What was the cause of the Great Potato Famine in Ireland in the 1800s?

_____

Section 19.4 STUDY GUIDE CONTINUED

Write where the different funguslike protists can be found, their ecological roles, and their possible body forms in the table below.

Funguslike Protist	Where Found	Ecological Role	Body Forms
Plasmodial slime mold	8.	decomposer	plasmodium, spore producing structure, spores that can move
Cellular slime mold	9.	10.	11.
Water mold	12.	13.	14.

Vocabulary Check

slime mold	water mold

_____ **15.** can grow as large as a meter or more

_____ **16.** has a resistant, resting stage

_____ **17.** can have a cottony appearance

_____ **18.** releases chemical signals that cause the cells to swarm together

Name Period Date

SECTION
19.5

DIVERSITY OF FUNGI
Study Guide

KEY CONCEPT
Fungi are heterotrophs that absorb their food.

VOCABULARY	
chitin	fruiting body
hyphae	mycorrhizae
mycelium	sporangia

MAIN IDEA: Fungi are adapted to absorb their food from the environment

1. What are the three informal groups that fungi can be divided into?

____

2. What is one way that fungi are similar to insects?

____

In the chart below, compare fungi and plants.

Characteristics	Fungi	Plants
How do they get their food?	**3.**	**4.**
What structures make up their bodies?	hyphae, mycelium, fruiting body	**5.**
What makes up their cell walls?	**6.**	**7.**

CHAPTER 19
Protists and Fungi

Section 19.5 STUDY GUIDE CONTINUED

MAIN IDEA: Fungi come in many shapes and sizes.

Sketch and label an example of each of the following: sac fungi, bread mold, and club fungi.
Pick figures throughout the chapter as examples for your sketches.

8. Sac Fungus	9. Bread Mold	10. Club Fungus

MAIN IDEA: Fungi reproduce sexually and asexually.

11. List the three ways that yeast can reproduce.

_____

12. Why are single-celled yeasts classified as sac fungi?

_____

13. Where can the reproductive structures of a club fungi, called basidia, be found on a mushroom?

_____

Vocabulary Check

_____ **14.** spore-forming structures of fungi

_____ **15.** aboveground reproductive structure of a fungus

_____ **16.** a tough polysaccharide that makes up the cell walls of fungi

_____ **17.** symbiotic relationship between plant roots and fungi

_____ **18.** long strands that make up the bodies of multicellular fungi

_____ **19.** a tangled mass of hyphae

ECOLOGY OF FUNGI
Study Guide

KEY CONCEPT
Fungi recycle nutrients in the environment.

VOCABULARY
lichen

MAIN IDEA: Fungi may be decomposers, pathogens, or mutualists.

1. How does the decomposing activity of fungi help ecosystems?

   _____

2. How are fungi well adapted as decomposers?

   _____

3. Fungi are the main decomposers of what two tough plant materials?

   _____

4. What negative effect to human industry may fungi decomposers have?

   _____

5. What are organisms that always cause disease called?

   _____

6. How does overuse or incorrect use of antibiotics contribute to infection by fungi?

   _____

7. What are two fairly mild infections to humans that are caused by fungi?

   _____

8. What are three diseases of plants that are caused by fungi?

   _____

9. What is usually the source of the chemicals used in antifungal medicines?

   _____

10. Use Figure 19.27 to sketch and label the structure of a lichen in the space provided.

Section 19.6 STUDY GUIDE CONTINUED

11. What does an associated alga provide to a lichen?

_____

12. What two roles do lichens play in an ecosystem?

_____

13. Mycorrhizae are mutualistic associations between plant roots and fungi. What does the fungi provide in this relationship?

_____

14. How does the fungus benefit by being associated with plant roots as mycorrhizae?

_____

15. What are two ways mycorrhizae are beneficial to a plant?

_____

MAIN IDEA: **Fungi are studied for many purposes.**
Fill in the concept map below with details of how humans use fungi for different purposes.

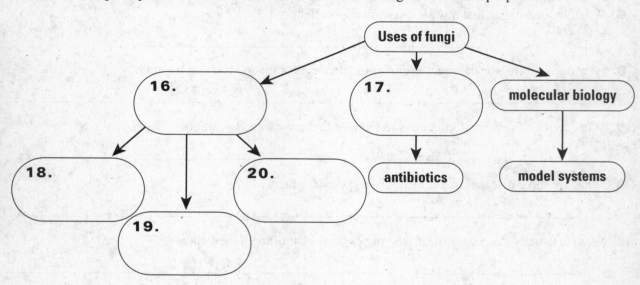

Vocabulary Check
21. A lichen is a mutualistic relationship between what two types of organisms?

_____

SECTION 20.1 | ORIGINS OF PLANT LIFE
Study Guide

KEY CONCEPT
Plant life began in the water and became adapted to land.

VOCABULARY		
plant	vascular system	seed
cuticle	lignin	
stomata	pollen grain	

MAIN IDEA: **Land plants evolved from green algae.**

1. Name five characteristics that green algae and land plants share.

   _____

   _____

2. The common ancestor of all plants would be classified in what class if it were alive today?

   _____

3. What plant characteristics probably originated in charophyceans?

   _____

   _____

MAIN IDEA: **Plants have adaptations that allow them to live on land.**

In the table below, take notes about the challenges that plants face on land and adaptations to these challenges.

Challenge	Description	Adaptations
4. retaining moisture		
5. transporting resources		
6. growing upright		
7. reproducing on land		

Section 20.1 STUDY GUIDE CONTINUED

CHAPTER 20
Plant Diversity

MAIN IDEA: Plants evolve with other organisms in their environment.

8. Give two examples of mutualisms that have evolved between plants and other types of organisms.

_____

_____

9. Give two examples of how plants have evolved with the animals that eat them.

_____

_____

Vocabulary Check

In the spaces provided below, draw pictures that help you to remember the definitions of the vocabulary words.

Plant	Vascular system

Cuticle and stomata	Seed

SECTION 20.2 | CLASSIFICATION OF PLANTS
Study Guide

KEY CONCEPT

Plants can be classified into nine phyla.

VOCABULARY		
pollination	angiosperm	flower
gymnosperm	cone	fruit

MAIN IDEA: Mosses and their relatives are seedless nonvascular plants.

1. What is required in order for seedless plants to reproduce?

2. How do nonvascular plants obtain water and nutrients?

3. Take notes about seedless nonvascular plants in the table below.

Plant Type	Phylum Name	Characteristics
liverworts		
hornworts		
mosses		

MAIN IDEA: Club mosses and ferns are seedless vascular plants.

4. How does having a vascular system affect how seedless vascular plants grow?

5. Take notes about seedless vascular plants in the table below.

Plant Type	Phylum Name	Characteristics
club mosses		
ferns		

Section 20.2 STUDY GUIDE CONTINUED

MAIN IDEA: **Seed plants include cone-bearing plants and flowering plants.**

6. What are three advantages that seed plants have over their seedless relatives?

_____

_____

7. Name and describe the two broad categories of seed plants.

_____

_____

8. Take notes about seed plants in the table below.

Plant Type	Phylum Name	Characteristics
cycads		
ginkgo		
conifers		
flowering plants		

Vocabulary Check

pollination	cone	flower	fruit

_____ **9.** mature ovary of flower

_____ **10.** process in which pollen meets female parts of same plant species

_____ **11.** reproductive structure of most gymnosperms

_____ **12.** reproductive structure of angiosperms

SECTION 20.3 | DIVERSITY OF FLOWERING PLANTS
Study Guide

KEY CONCEPT

The largest phylum in the plant kingdom is the flowering plants.

VOCABULARY	
cotyledon	dicot
monocot	wood

MAIN IDEA: Flowering plants have unique adaptations that allow them to dominate in today's world.

Fill in the concept map below about the adaptations of flowering plants.

Flowering plants

have → 1.

have → 3.

which can allow for more efficient → 2.

which plays a role in → 4.

MAIN IDEA: Botanists classify flowering plants into two groups based on seed type.

Take notes about monocots and dicots in the table below.

Type of Flowering Plant	Number of Cotyledons	Other Characteristics
5. monocot		
6. dicot		

MAIN IDEA: Flowering plants are also categorized by stem type and lifespan.

7. Why is it helpful to categorize flowering plants in ways other than by seed type?

_____

_____

8. Describe the two major stem types of flowering plants.

_____

_____

9. Take notes about the three lifespan types of flowering plants.

Lifespan	Characteristics	Examples
annual		
biennial		
perennial		

Vocabulary Check

10. What is a cotyledon?

_____

11. How does the prefix *mono-,* meaning "one," relate to the meaning of *monocot*?

_____

12. How does the prefix *di-,* meaning "two," relate to the meaning of *dicot*?

_____

13. What is wood made up of?

_____

**SECTION
20.4**

PLANTS IN HUMAN CULTURE
Study Guide

KEY CONCEPT
Humans rely on plants in many ways.

VOCABULARY	
botany	pharmacology
ethnobotany	alkaloid

MAIN IDEA: **Agriculture provides stable food supplies for people in permanent settlements.**

1. How have people obtained food for the majority of human history?

_____

2. How have farmers "tamed" wild crop species over the past 10,000 years?

_____

_____

3. How has farming become part of a culture's economy?

_____

_____

Take notes about the requirements and benefits of the following methods of obtaining food.

Method	Requirements	Benefits
4. hunting and gathering		
5. agriculture		

Section 20.4 STUDY GUIDE CONTINUED

MAIN IDEA: **Plant products are important economic resources.**

6. How were plants involved in the great seafaring expeditions of the 1400s and 1500s?

_____

_____

7. Name three plant products that are important to the global economy today.

_____

MAIN IDEA: **Plant compounds are essential to modern medicine.**

Fill in the main idea web below with notes about the role of plants in modern medicine.

Pharmacology:	Alkaloids:

Main Idea: Plant compounds are essential to modern medicine.

Role of plants:	Synthetic drugs:

Vocabulary Check

botany	ethnobotany	pharmacology

_____ **8.** study of plants

_____ **9.** study of drugs and their effects on the body

_____ **10.** study of how people use plants

SECTION 21.1 | PLANT CELLS AND TISSUES
Study Guide

KEY CONCEPT
Plants have specialized cells and tissue systems.

VOCABULARY		
parenchyma cell	dermal tissue	xylem
collenchyma cell	ground tissue	phloem
sclerenchyma cell	vascular tissue	

MAIN IDEA: **Plant tissues are made of three basic cell types.**

Write the functions of each of the three basic cell types, and sketch or describe their appearance in the chart below.

Cell Type	Function	Sketch or Description
1. Parenchyma cell		
2. Collenchyma cell		
3. Sclerenchyma cell		

Section 21.1 STUDY GUIDE CONTINUED

MAIN IDEA: Plant organs are made of three tissue systems.

Fill in the concept map below with supporting details about the three tissue systems of plants.

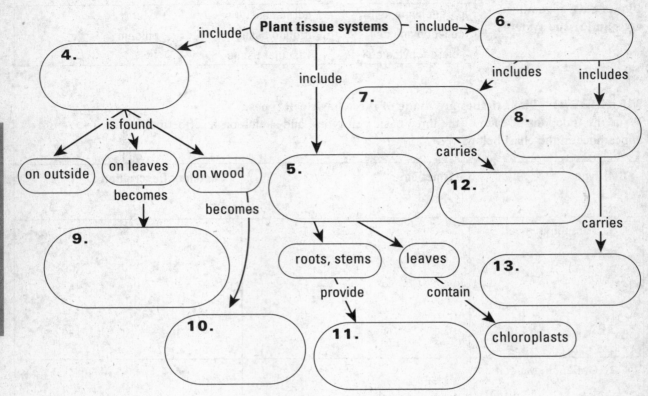

Vocabulary Check

parenchyma cell	sclerenchyma cell	ground tissue	xylem
collencyhma cell	dermal tissue	vascular tissue	phloem

_____ **14.** Outer covering of a plant

_____ **15.** Includes xylem and phloem

_____ **16.** Tissue that makes up the majority of a plant

_____ **17.** Supporting cell type that makes up celery strands

_____ **18.** Vascular tissue that carries sugars

_____ **19.** Strongest cell type that makes up fruit pits

_____ **20.** Most common cell type that can help plants heal from injury

_____ **21.** Vascular tissue that carries water and dissolved minerals

SECTION 21.2 | THE VASCULAR SYSTEM
Study Guide

KEY CONCEPT

The vascular system allows for the transport of water, minerals, and sugars.

VOCABULARY
cohesion-tension theory
transpiration
pressure-flow model

MAIN IDEA: Water and dissolved minerals move through xylem.

The cohesion-tension theory proposes that the physical properties of water allow the rise of water through a plant. Sketch and describe cohesion and adhesion of water molecules.

1. Cohesion
Sketch:
Description:

2. Adhesion
Sketch:
Description:

Fill in the sequence diagram below to explain how water moves through the roots, stems, and leaves of a plant within xylem. Use the text and Figure 21.4 to help fill in the diagram.

3. Roots	→	4. Stems	→	5. Leaves

MAIN IDEA: **Phloem carries sugars from photosynthesis throughout the plant.**

6. Phloem sap moves from a sugar source to a sugar sink. What are two plant parts that might be sources of sugars?

_____

7. What is a sugar sink in a plant?

_____

8. The pressure changes between sugar sources and sinks keeps sap flowing through phloem. Is there a higher concentration of sugars at a sugar source or a sugar sink?

_____

9. In the movement of sap through phloem, what two events require energy on the part of the plant?

_____

10. Water moves into the phloem due to the high sugar concentration there. It requires no energy. What is this process called?

_____

Vocabulary Check

cohesion-tension theory	pressure-flow model	transpiration

_____ 11. Well-supported theory that describes how sugars move through a plant within phloem

_____ 12. Well-supported theory that describes how water and dissolved minerals move through a plant within xylem

_____ 13. Term that describes how water moves through a plant within xylem by evaporation from leaves

SECTION
21.3 | ROOTS AND STEMS
Study Guide

KEY CONCEPT

Roots and stems form the support system of vascular plants.

VOCABULARY		
vascular cylinder	meristem	primary growth
root hair	fibrous root	secondary growth
root cap	taproot	

MAIN IDEA: **Roots anchor plants and absorb mineral nutrients from soil.**

In the space provided, sketch a root tip. Draw lines from the terms to label the sketch, and describe the function for each of the parts. Use Figure 21.7 and the text to fill in the diagram.

Sketch:

1. Vascular cylinder _____

_____

_____

2. Apical meristem _____

_____

_____

3. Root cap _____

_____

_____

4. How do root hairs help a plant?

_____

5. What are root systems made of fine branches of about the same size called?

_____

6. What are root systems that have one main root and can sometimes store food called?

_____

7. Plants are not just soaking up water. They use energy to absorb _____ .

8. The increased concentration of ions in root cells causes _____ to move

into the root.

9. An example of a mineral needed in large amounts is _____.

10. Other minerals, such as _____ , are needed in small amounts.

Section 21.3 STUDY GUIDE CONTINUED

MAIN IDEA: Stems support plants, transport materials, and provide storage.

11. What are three functions of most stems?

_____

12. Look at Figure 21.10. What are two plants whose stems store water?

_____

13. What special adaptation do strawberry plant stems have?

_____

14. What are two stems that grow underground?

_____

15. What are four characteristics of herbaceous stems?

_____

_____

16. What is growth that makes stems grow taller or roots grow longer called?

_____

17. What is growth that makes stems and roots of woody plants grow wider called?

_____

18. What represents one year of growth on a tree ring?

_____

Vocabulary Check

_____ **19.** Tough covering on root tip

_____ **20.** Unspecialized tissue of dividing cells

_____ **21.** Houses xylem and phloem

_____ **22.** Root system made of equal-sized roots

_____ **23.** Growth pattern that increases height and length

_____ **24.** Increases surface area of a root

_____ **25.** Root system that reaches deep into the ground

_____ **26.** Growth pattern that increases width

SECTION 21.4 | LEAVES
Study Guide

KEY CONCEPT
Leaves absorb light and carry out photosynthesis.

VOCABULARY	
blade	mesophyll
petiole	guard cell

MAIN IDEA: Most leaves share similar structures.

1. Sketch a leaf attached to a stem. Label the blade, petiole, stem, and axillary bud.

Use a sequence diagram to fill in the steps describing how stomata regulate gas exchange.

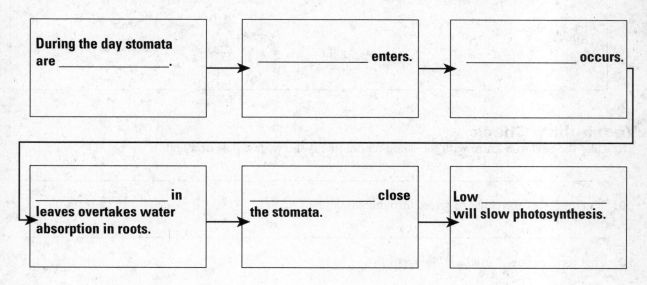

During the day stomata are _____.	→	_____ enters.	→	_____ occurs.

_____ in leaves overtakes water absorption in roots.	→	_____ close the stomata.	→	Low _____ will slow photosynthesis.

2. What are three leaf characteristics that can be used for plant identification?

_____

3. How can you tell the difference between a leaf and a leaflet?

_____

Section 21.4 STUDY GUIDE CONTINUED

MAIN IDEA: **Most leaves are specialized systems for photosynthesis.**

4. What is the photosynthetic tissue of a leaf?

_____

5. How are the two types of mesophyll found in a leaf specialized for photosynthesis?

_____

_____

6. What are three adaptations of plants that help reduce water loss in a desert or cold environment?

_____

_____

7. Use the following terms and stack them like you were building a sandwich in the order they are found within a leaf: mesophyll, dermal tissue, dermal tissue, cuticle, cuticle.

Vocabulary Check

8. Like the part of a knife with the same name, this is the widest part of a leaf.

_____

9. "Guards" the exchange of gases through stomata

_____

10. This term means "stalk" or "leafstalk."

_____

11. This term means "middle leaf," which is where it is found.

_____

22.1 | PLANT LIFE CYCLES
Study Guide

KEY CONCEPT
All plants alternate between two phases in their life cycles.

VOCABULARY	
alternation of generations	gametophyte
sporophyte	

MAIN IDEA: Plant life cycles alternate between producing spores and gametes.

1. What is the alternation of generations?

   _____

2. What are the characteristics of a sporophyte and a gametophyte?

   _____

   _____

3. At what point is meiosis involved in the plant life cycle?

   _____

fertilization	sporophyte	spores	gametes
zygote	meiosis	gametophyte	

4. Use Figure 22.1 to draw a diagram illustrating the alternation of generations in plants. Be sure to use all of the words in the word box above as labels in your diagram.

Section 22.1 STUDY GUIDE CONTINUED

MAIN IDEA: Life cycle phases look different among various plant groups.

Fill in the table below with notes about alternation of generations in different plant groups.

Plant Group	Example	Sporophyte	Gametophyte
5. nonvascular plants			
6. seedless vascular plants			
7. seed plants			

Vocabulary Check

8. What two phases alternate, or pass back and forth, in the alternation of generations?

_____

9. How is the word part *sporo* related to the meaning of *sporophyte*?

_____

10. How is the word part *gameto* related to the meaning of *gametophyte*?

_____

SECTION
22.2

REPRODUCTION IN FLOWERING PLANTS
Study Guide

KEY CONCEPT

Reproduction of flowering plants takes place within flowers.

VOCABULARY		
sepal	carpel	double fertilization
petal	ovary	
stamen	endosperm	

MAIN IDEA: **Flowers contain reproductive organs protected by specialized leaves.**

1. Use Figure 22.5 to draw a diagram of a flower. Be sure to use all of the words in the word box below as labels in your diagram. Write the functions of the sepal, petal, stamen, and carpel next their labels.

sepal	stamen: filament, anther
petal	carpel: stigma, style, ovary

MAIN IDEA: **Flowering plants can be pollinated by wind or animals.**

2. What needs to happen for a flowering plant to be pollinated?

_____

3. Why is animal pollination more efficient than wind pollination?

_____

_____

Section 22.2 STUDY GUIDE CONTINUED

MAIN IDEA: Fertilization takes place within the flower.

Take notes about the processes involved in the reproduction of flowering plants.

Process	How It Works	Products/Results
4. production of male gametes		
5. production of female gametes		
6. double fertilization		
7. development of fruit and seeds		

Vocabulary Check

8. *Ovum* is the Latin word meaning "egg." How is this meaning related to the words *ovary* and *ovule*?

_____

9. What two structures are "fertilized" during double fertilization?

_____

SECTION 22.3

SEED DISPERSAL AND GERMINATION
Study Guide

KEY CONCEPT

Seeds disperse and begin to grow when conditions are favorable.

VOCABULARY

dormancy   germination

MAIN IDEA: Animals, wind, and water can spread seeds.

1. What is the function of fruit in flowering plants?

_____

2. Why is seed dispersal important?

_____

_____

3. Describe two ways that seeds can be spread by animals.

_____

_____

4. What fruit forms can allow seeds to be spread by wind and water?

_____

_____

MAIN IDEA: Seeds begin to grow when environmental conditions are favorable.

5. When a seed is _____, the embryo has stopped growing.

6. Seed dormancy allows the next generation of plants to grow under

_____ conditions.

7. What types of conditions can end dormancy for many plant species?

_____

8. Take notes about germination in this cause-and-effect chart.

Cause	→	Effect(s)
embryo takes up water		
water activates enzymes		
sugars are moved to embryo		

9. Describe the order in which seedling structures emerge during germination.

_____

_____

10. At what stage in development is a young plant considered a seedling?

_____

Vocabulary Check

11. Hibernation is to an animal as _____ is to a seed.

12. How does the Latin word *germen,* meaning "seed," relate to the meaning of *germination*?

_____

SECTION 22.4 | ASEXUAL REPRODUCTION
Study Guide

KEY CONCEPT
Plants can produce genetic clones of themselves through asexual reproduction.

VOCABULARY
regeneration
vegetative reproduction

MAIN IDEA: Plants can reproduce asexually with stems, leaves, or roots.

1. What is asexual reproduction?

_____

2. How can the ability to reproduce asexually help plants to populate a variety of environments?

_____

_____

Take notes about plant reproduction in the concept map below.

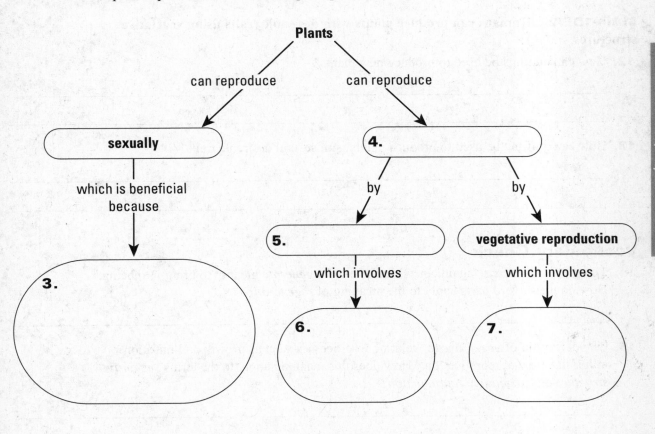

Section 22.4 STUDY GUIDE CONTINUED

Fill in the chart with notes about structures adapted for vegetative reproduction.

Structure	Description	How It Works	Example
8. stolon			
9. rhizome			
10. tuber			
11. bulb			

MAIN IDEA: **Humans can produce plants with desirable traits using vegetative structures.**

12. How can cuttings be used to produce new plants?

_____

_____

13. How can grafting be used to produce plants with several desirable traits?

_____

_____

Vocabulary Check

14. The prefix *re-* means "again; anew" and the word *generate* means "to bring into being." How do these word parts apply to the meaning of *regeneration*?

_____

15. One definition of *vegetative* is "relating to processes such as growth and nutrition rather than sexual reproduction." How does this meaning apply to the terms *vegetative structure* and *vegetative reproduction*?

_____

_____

SECTION 22.5 | PLANT HORMONES AND RESPONSES
Study Guide

KEY CONCEPT
Plant hormones guide plant growth and development.

VOCABULARY

hormone	auxin	gravitropism
gibberellin	tropism	photoperiodism
ethylene	phototropism	
cytokinin	thigmotropism	

MAIN IDEA: Plant hormones regulate plant functions.

1. What is a hormone?

_____

_____

2. Give two reasons why plant hormones may be released.

_____

_____

Take notes about the four main groups of plant hormones in the chart below.

Plant Hormone	Processes Involved In
3. gibberellins	
4. ethylene	
5. cytokinins	
6. auxins	

CHAPTER 22
Plant Growth, Reproduction

MAIN IDEA: **Plants can respond to light, touch, gravity, and seasonal changes.**
Match the term from the word box with the correct description.

phototropism	thigmotropism	gravitropism	rapid response	photoperiodism

_____ **7.** Growth in response to being touched

_____ **8.** Response to being touched not involving growth

_____ **9.** Growth in response to gravity

_____ **10.** Response to changing lengths of day and night

_____ **11.** Growth in response to light

Vocabulary Check

12. The prefixes *photo-, thigmo-,* and *gravi-* refer to light, touch, and gravity, and the Greek
word *trope* means "a turning." How do these word parts relate to the meanings of
phototropism, thigmotropism, and *gravitropism*?

_____

_____

13. In the space provided below, illustrate the process of phototropism as it occurs at the
cellular level. Use Figure 22.16 as a reference. Be sure to label areas of high auxin
concentration.

SECTION
23.1 | ANIMAL CHARACTERISTICS
Study Guide

KEY CONCEPT
Animals are diverse but share common characteristics.

VOCABULARY
collagen
homeotic
homeobox

MAIN IDEA: **Animals are the most physically diverse kingdom of organisms.**

1. Give three examples that support the statement that animals are a remarkably diverse group of organisms.

_____

_____

MAIN IDEA: **All animals share a common set of characteristics.**

2. Complete the following main idea web with details about the common characteristics shared by all animals.

```
┌──────────────────────┐        ┌──────────────────────┐
│                      │        │                      │
│                      │        │                      │
│                      │        │                      │
└──────────────────────┘        └──────────────────────┘
            \                      /
             ┌────────────────────────────┐
             │                            │
             │   Animal characteristics   │
             │                            │
             └────────────────────────────┘
            /                      \
┌──────────────────────┐        ┌──────────────────────┐
│                      │        │                      │
│                      │        │                      │
└──────────────────────┘        └──────────────────────┘
```

Section 23.1 STUDY GUIDE CONTINUED

3. How are animal cells different from plant cells?

_____

_____

_____

4. Explain how *Hox* genes influence animal development.

_____

_____

_____

Vocabulary Check

5. What is collagen?

_____

6. What is the connection between homeotic and homeobox (*Hox*) genes?

_____

_____

Be Creative

7. In the box below, design a poster that celebrates animal diversity.

```



```

SECTION
23.2
ANIMAL DIVERSITY
Study Guide

KEY CONCEPT
More than 95 percent of all animal species are invertebrates.

VOCABULARY	
vertebrate	radial symmetry
invertebrate	protostome
phylum	deuterostome
bilateral symmetry	

MAIN IDEA: Each animal phylum has a unique body plan.

Use your textbook to fill in the missing words in the following sentences.

1. A vertebrate is an animal with an internal segmented _____. Vertebrates make up less than _____ percent of all known animal species.

2. Invertebrates are animals without _____. Invertebrates make up over _____ percent of all known animal species.

3. Animals are divided into more than 30 major groups, which are called _____. Each group of animals is defined by _____ and _____ characteristics.

4. Differences in body plans result from differences in the expression of _____ genes.

5. What is the function of a homeobox gene?

_____

_____

6. What is the connection between *Hox* genes and the diversity of animal body plans?

_____

_____

7. What factor might account for the development of so many unique body plans during the Cambrian explosion?

_____

_____

Section 23.2 STUDY GUIDE CONTINUED

CHAPTER 23
Invertebrate Diversity

MAIN IDEA: Animals are grouped using a variety of criteria.

For each type of symmetry, write a short description, and sketch a picture of an animal that exhibits each type of symmetry.

Symmetry	Description	Sketch
8. bilateral		
9. radial		

10. What are three differences in the developmental patterns of protostomes and deuterostomes?

_____

_____

_____

Vocabulary Check

11. What is a phylum?

_____

_____

12. If *stoma* means "mouth," what do you think *proto-* and *deutero-* mean?

_____

_____

SECTION 23.3 | SPONGES AND CNIDARIANS
Study Guide

KEY CONCEPT

Sponges and cnidarians are the simplest animals.

VOCABULARY		
sessile	medusa	gastrovascular cavity
filter feeder	mesoglea	
polyp	nematocyst	

MAIN IDEA: Sponges have specialized cells but no tissues.

Choose the correct term or terms from the box below to complete the following sentences.

muscle	sessile	toxic	predators
nerve	hard	growing	parasites

1. Sponges lack _____ and _____ cells. They are _____, meaning

   they are unable to move from where they are attached.

2. Sponges attach to _____ surfaces. They secrete _____ substances that

   keep other sponges from _____ into their area and also protect them from

   _____ and _____.

3. Explain the difference between sexual and asexual reproduction in sponges.

   _____

   _____

4. How does a sponge filter feed?

   _____

   _____

5. Describe the anatomy of a sponge.

   _____

   _____

6. List and describe the three types of cells that make up a sponge.

   _____

   _____

Section 23.3 STUDY GUIDE CONTINUED

MAIN IDEA: Cnidarians are the oldest existing animals that have specialized tissues.

Complete the following chart with a description and simple sketch of the two types of cnidarian body types.

Body Form	Description	Sketch
7. polyp		
8. medusa		

9. How do cnidarians reproduce asexually?

_____

_____

Choose the correct term from the box to fit each definition of a part of a cnidarian's anatomy.

| cnidocytes | contracting cells | mesoglea | nerve cells |

_____ **10.** These cells interconnect and form a network over the entire animal. They send sensory information around the animal and coordinate muscular contractions.

_____ **11.** This is a non-cellular jellylike material.

_____ **12.** These cells cover the surface of a cnidarian and contain muscle fibers.

_____ **13.** These cells contain stinging structures used for defense and capturing prey.

Vocabulary Check

14. What is a nematocyst?

_____

15. What is the function of the gastrovascular cavity?

_____

SECTION FLATWORMS, MOLLUSKS, AND ANNELIDS
23.4 | Study Guide

KEY CONCEPT
Flatworms, mollusks, and annelids
belong to closely related phyla.

VOCABULARY		
complete digestive tract	hemocoel	coelom
radula	segmentation	

MAIN IDEA: Flatworms are simple bilateral animals.

1. Flatworms, mollusks, and annelids are members of which phylum?

_____

2. Describe the basic body plan of a flatworm.

_____

_____

3. Why are flatworms flat?

_____

_____

4. What are the three classes of flatworms?

_____

5. What is schistosomiasis?

_____

_____

6. Describe the life cycle of a tapeworm.

_____

_____

_____

_____

Section 23.4 STUDY GUIDE CONTINUED

MAIN IDEA: **Mollusks are diverse animals.**

7. What is a complete digestive tract?

_____

_____

8. What is a benefit of having a complete digestive tract?

_____

_____

9. Complete the following chart with a description of each of the three shared anatomical features of mollusks.

Anatomical Feature	Description
radula	
mantle	
ctenidia	

10. What is a hemocoel?

_____

_____

MAIN IDEA: **Annelids have segmented bodies.**

11. What are the three groups of annelids?

_____

Vocabulary Check

12. The word *coelom* comes from a Greek word that means "cavity." How does this word origin relate to the definition of a coelom?

_____

SECTION
23.5 ROUNDWORMS
Study Guide

KEY CONCEPT
Roundworms have bilateral symmetry and shed their outer skeleton to grow.

VOCABULARY
cuticle
pseudocoelom

MAIN IDEA: Roundworms shed their stiff outer skeleton as they grow.
Use words from the box below to complete the following sentences.

bilateral	cuticle	nematodes	protostomes
chitin	diversity	numbers	shed
	exoskeleton		

1. Roundworms, or _____, are one of the most numerous kinds of animals,

   both in terms of _____ and in terms of species _____.

2. Members of the Ecdysozoa are _____ (meaning their gut cavity forms

   mouth-first) and they have _____ symmetry.

3. All Ecdysozoans have a tough _____ called a _____.

4. The cuticle is made of _____ and must be _____

   whenever the animal grows larger.

5. Describe the anatomy of a roundworm.

   _____

   _____

   _____

MAIN IDEA: Many roundworms are parasites.
Complete the following chart with information about parasitic roundworms.

Parasite	Where Found?	Infections Occur By:
6. hookworm		

Parasite	Where Found?	Infections Occur By:
7. pinworm		
8. Guinea worm		

Vocabulary Check

9. The prefix *pseudo-* comes from a Greek word which means "false." For example, the term *pseudoscience* refers to a theory, method, or practice that is considered to lack a foundation in scientific principles; it is false science. How does the meaning of *pseudo* relate to the definition of a pseudocoelom?

_____

_____

Be Creative

Design a poster that tells people how to avoid parasitic roundworm infections. Your design can focus on just one type of roundworm or more if you choose.

**SECTION
23.6** | ECHINODERMS
Study Guide

KEY CONCEPT

Echinoderms are on the same evolutionary branch as vertebrates.

VOCABULARY
ossicle
water vascular system

MAIN IDEA: Echinoderms have radial symmetry.

Use words from the box below to complete the following sentences.

arm	flexible	ossicles	stiff
catch connective	internal	ring canal	water

1. All echinoderms have an _____ skeleton made up of many tiny

   interlocking calcium-based plates called _____.

2. The plates are joined together by a unique _____ _____

   tissue with adjustable stiffness.

3. This tissue lets echinoderms change their consistency, going from very

   _____ to very _____ in a matter of seconds.

4. A water vascular system is a series of _____-filled canals that extend

   along each _____ from the _____ _____

   surrounding the central disk.

5. What is the function of the water vascular system?

   _____

   _____

   _____

   _____

6. Describe how a sea star eats a clam.

   _____

   _____

   _____

   _____

MAIN IDEA: There are five classes of Echinoderms.

Complete the following chart with information about each Echinoderm class.

Class	Description	Example
7. Crinoidea		
8. Asteroidea		
9. Ophiuriodea		
10. Echinoidea		
11. Holothuroidea		

Vocabulary Check

12. The term *ossicle* comes from a Latin word meaning "bone." How does this word origin relate to the definition of an ossicle?

_____

Be Creative

Create an informative brochure for a tide pool. Include information about all the different kinds of echinoderms a visitor would find there.

Name Period Date

SECTION
24.1 ARTHROPOD DIVERSITY
Study Guide

KEY CONCEPT
Arthropods are the most diverse of all animals.

VOCABULARY		
arthropod	chitin	segmentation
exoskeleton	appendage	

MAIN IDEA: Arthropod features are highly adapted.

1. What are the three main features of an arthropod's body?

____

2. What is chitin?

____

3. Why are jointed appendages considered an important adaptation during the evolution of arthropods?

____

____

4. Complete the following chart with a description of and example animal for each group of arthropods.

Group	Description	Example
trilobites		
crustaceans		
chelicerates		
insects		
myriapods		

CHAPTER 24
A Closer Look at Arthropods

MAIN IDEA: Arthropod exoskeletons serve a variety of functions.

5. What three important body functions that are made difficult by the presence of an exoskeleton?

_____

6. Why must an arthropod molt?

_____

7. List the three steps of the molting process.

_____

_____

_____

8. How is an arthropod's circulatory system different from a vertebrate's circulatory system?

_____

9. What body parts allow an arthropod to sense its surrounding environment?

_____

_____

10. How is an arthropod's eye different from a mammal's eye?

_____

_____

MAIN IDEA: Arthropod diversity evolved over millions of years.

11. What two species do scientists think are the closest relatives to arthropods?

_____

Vocabulary Check

12. The word *appendage* comes from the Latin word *appendere*, which means "to hang upon." How does this meaning relate to the definition of appendage?

_____

13. What word within *segmentation* helps you remember it as something made of separate parts?

_____

SECTION
24.2
CRUSTACEANS
Study Guide

KEY CONCEPT

Crustaceans are a diverse group of ancient arthropods.

VOCABULARY		
crustacean	abdomen	mandible
cephalothorax	carapace	

MAIN IDEA: **Crustaceans evolved as marine arthropods.**

1. What are the four main features of a crustacean's body?

_____

_____

Choose a word from the box below that best fits each of the following descriptions.

abdomen	carapace	cephalothorax

_____ 2. This body section is the region of an organism in which the head and trunk region are combined into one long section

_____ 3. This body section refers to the rear portion of the organism.

_____ 4. This shieldlike section of cuticle covers the sides of the body and protects the gills.

MAIN IDEA: **Crustacean appendages can take many forms.**

5. List three functions of a crustacean claw.

_____

_____

6. What is the function of a crustacean's antennae?

_____

7. What are mandibles?

_____

8. What two body parts are used by a crustacean to move?

_____

Section 24.2 STUDY GUIDE CONTINUED

9. In the space below, draw a simple sketch of a crustacean and label its parts.

MAIN IDEA: There are many different types of crustaceans.

10. Complete the following chart with a description of each crustacean group.

Group	Description
decapod	
barnacle	
isopod	
tongue worm	

11. What evidence helped to determine that barnacles and tongue worms are crustaceans?

_____

Vocabulary Check

12. The word *mandible* comes from the Latin word *mandere*, which means "to chew." How does this meaning relate to the definition of mandibles?

_____

SECTION 24.3 | ARACHNIDS
Study Guide

KEY CONCEPT
Arachnids include spiders and their relatives.

VOCABULARY		
chelicerate	book lung	trachea
arachnid	spiracle	

MAIN IDEA: Arachnids are the largest group of chelicerates.

1. What is a chelicerate?

_____

2. What are three characteristics of arachnids?

_____

Choose a word from the word box below that best fits each of the following descriptions.

book lungs	Malpighian tubules	spiracles	tracheae

_____ **3.** tiny holes on the abdomen that open and close to allow oxygen to enter

_____ **4.** structures built of many thin, hollow sheets of tissue

_____ **5.** tubes that carry oxygen directly to the arachnid's tissues

_____ **6.** excretory structures that allow spiders to minimize loss of water while excreting metabolic wastes

7. In the space below, draw a simple picture of a spider and label its parts.

Section 24.3 STUDY GUIDE CONTINUED

MAIN IDEA: Arachnids have evolved into a diverse group.

8. Where is silk produced in a spider's body?

_____

9. List four uses of a spider's silk.

_____

_____

10. What is the function of a spider's venom?

_____

11. List one positive and one negative aspect of an arachnid's role as a predator.

_____

Vocabulary Check

12. The word *spiracle* comes from the Latin word *spirare*, which means "to breathe." Explain how this meaning relates to the definition of a spiracle.

_____

Be Creative

13. Draw a cartoon that illustrates the importance of spiders as predators.

SECTION
24.4

INSECT ADAPTATIONS
Study Guide

KEY CONCEPT
Insects show an amazing range of adaptations.

VOCABULARY

incomplete metamorphosis

complete metamorphosis

pupa

MAIN IDEA: **Insects are the dominant terrestrial arthropods.**

1. Explain why insects are considered an incredible success story.

_____

_____

2. Draw a picture of an insect and label the following parts: head, thorax, abdomen, legs, wings, antennae, and compound eyes.

MAIN IDEA: **Insects undergo metamorphosis.**

3. Describe incomplete metamorphosis.

_____

_____

Section 24.4 STUDY GUIDE CONTINUED

4. Complete the following process diagram with details about the complete metamorphosis of a butterfly.

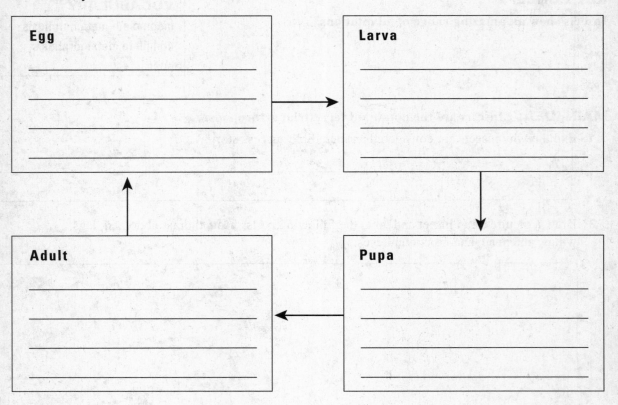

MAIN IDEA: Insects have adapted to life on land.

For each type of insect, indicate whether it uses a *proboscis* or *mandibles* to eat.

_____ **5.** butterfly

_____ **6.** ant

_____ **7.** beetle

_____ **8.** moth

Vocabulary Check

9. What happens during a metamorphosis?

_____

10. What is the difference between complete and incomplete metamorphosis?

_____

SECTION 24.5 | ARTHROPODS AND HUMANS
Study Guide

KEY CONCEPT
Arthropods and humans interact in many ways.

> **VOCABULARY**
> insecticide
> vector

MAIN IDEA: **Arthropods and humans share many of the same resources.**

1. In what way do arthropods compete with humans for resources?

_____

_____

2. What is an insecticide?

_____

3. What are three negative aspects of insecticide use?

_____

_____

4. List and describe three safer methods scientists have developed to control insects.

_____

_____

_____

MAIN IDEA: **Some arthropods can spread human diseases.**

5. What is a vector?

_____

_____

CHAPTER 24
A Closer Look at Arthropods

Section 24.5 STUDY GUIDE CONTINUED

6. Complete the following chart with details about the following diseases transmitted to humans by arthropods.

Disease	Vector	Description
bubonic plague		
yellow fever		
malaria		
West Nile virus		

Vocabulary Check

7. The suffix *-cide* comes from the Latin word *caedere*, which means "to strike, kill." How does this meaning relate to the meaning of the word *insecticide*?

_____

8. *Vector* comes from the Latin word *vectus*, which means "to carry." Explain how this meaning relates to the definition of a vector.

_____

Be Creative

9. Draw a cartoon that illustrates the world through an insect's eyes. How might an insect see the world differently than you do? .

SECTION
25.1

VERTEBRATE ORIGINS
Study Guide

KEY CONCEPT
All vertebrates share common characteristics.

VOCABULARY
chordate
notochord
endoskeleton

MAIN IDEA: The phylum Chordata contains all vertebrates and some invertebrates.

1. What three groups make up the phylum Chordata?

_____

_____

Choose the correct term from the box below to fit each description.

notochord	hollow nerve cord	pharyngeal slits	tail

_____ **2.** extends beyond the anal opening, and contains segments of muscle tissue used for movement

_____ **3.** runs along the animal's back, forms from a section of ectoderm

_____ **4.** slits through the body wall in the pharynx

_____ **5.** flexible skeletal support rod embedded in the animal's back

MAIN IDEA: All vertebrates share common features.

6. What is an endoskeleton?

_____

_____

7. How does the growth of an animal with an endoskeleton differ from the growth of an animal with an exoskeleton?

_____

_____

_____

Section 25.1 STUDY GUIDE CONTINUED

Complete the following chart with the missing information for each vertebrate class.

Class	Description	Example
8. Agnatha		
9. Chondrichthyes		
10. Osteichthyes		
11. Amphibia		
12. Reptilia		
13. Aves		
14. Mammalia		

MAIN IDEA: Fossil evidence sheds light on the origins of vertebrates.

15. Where has most of the early vertebrate fossil evidence been found?

_____

16. Which animals are recognized as the first vertebrates?

_____

17. Which two groups of jawless fish still exist today?

_____

Vocabulary Check

18. The prefix *endo-* means "inside," while the prefix *exo-* means "outside." How does this help you to distinguish between an endoskeleton and an exoskeleton?

_____

_____

SECTION 25.2 | FISH DIVERSITY
Study Guide

KEY CONCEPT
The dominant aquatic vertebrates are fish.

VOCABULARY	
gill	lateral line
countercurrent flow	operculum

MAIN IDEA: Fish are vertebrates with gills and paired fins.

Choose a word or words from the box below to complete the following sentences.

blood	circulatory	gills	tissue
capillaries	countercurrent flow	opposite	

1. Fish use specialized organs called _____ to take in oxygen dissolved in water.

   Gills are large sheets of frilly _____ filled with _____.

2. Fish _____ systems pump blood in a single loop through a heart with two main

   chambers.

3. _____ _____ is the _____ movement of water against the flow of

   _____ in the fish's gills.

4. Explain how countercurrent flow works.

   _____

   _____

   _____

5. Draw a simple sketch of a fish and label the five main types of fins on its body.

MAIN IDEA: Jaws evolved from gill supports.

6. What are gill arches?

_____

7. What is an advantage of having jaws?

_____

MAIN IDEA: Only two groups of jawed fish still exist.

Use the box below to choose the correct word or words to complete the following sentences.

cartilage	electrical	lateral line	sensory
chimeras	Holocephali	muscular	sharks
Elasmobranchs	internal	rays	skates

8. Members of phylum Chondrichthyes have skeletons made of _____.

9. The two groups within phylum Chondrichthyes are the _____ and the

_____. The Holocephali include _____, also called ratfish. The

Elasmobranchs include _____, _____, and _____.

10. While the cartilaginous fish as a group may be ancient, they have many advanced

features. They have _____ fertilization, and many species give birth to live

young.

11. Fish can sense their prey's movements at a distance with a sensory system called the

_____.

12. Many fish also have _____ organs that detect the electrical currents made

by _____ contractions in other animals. These sensory organs are called

_____ cells because they receive electrical signals.

Vocabulary Check

13. The term *operculum* comes from a Latin word which means "to cover." Explain how
this meaning is related to the definition of an operculum.

_____

KEY CONCEPT
Bony fish include ray-finned and lobe-finned fish.

VOCABULARY	
ray-fin	lobe-fin
swim bladder	

MAIN IDEA: Ray-finned fish have a fan of bones in their fins.

1. Describe the shape of a ray-fin and list three reasons why its shape helps a ray-finned fish move.

   _____

   _____

2. Describe the diversity of ray-finned fish. How does the number of species of ray-finned fish compare to the total number of vertebrate species?

   _____

   _____

3. What is the function of the swim bladder?

   _____

MAIN IDEA: Lobe-finned fish have paired rounded fins supported by a single bone.

4. What is the evolutionary significance of lobe-finned fish?

   _____

   _____

   _____

5. Describe the structure of a lobe-fin.

   _____

   _____

CHAPTER 25
Vertebrate Diversity

Section 25.3 STUDY GUIDE CONTINUED

6. Complete the following Y-diagram to outline the similarities and differences between ray-fins and lobe-fins.

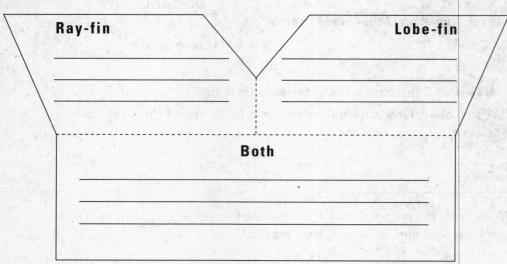

Ray-fin

Lobe-fin

Both

7. Name two types of lobe-finned fish that still exist today.

_____

Vocabulary Check

8. Use a comparison (for example, consider how a scuba diver travels to lower and higher depths) to describe how a swim bladder works.

_____

_____

_____

**SECTION
25.4** | AMPHIBIANS
Study Guide

KEY CONCEPT
Amphibians evolved from lobe-finned fish.

VOCABULARY

tetrapod	tadpole
amphibian	

MAIN IDEA: **Amphibians were the first animals with four limbs.**
Choose a word or words from the box below to complete the following sentences.

amphibians	four	land	water	vertebrate

1. A tetrapod is a _____ that has _____ limbs.

2. _____ are animals that can live both on _____ and in

_____.

3. Complete the following concept map with information about amphibian adaptations.

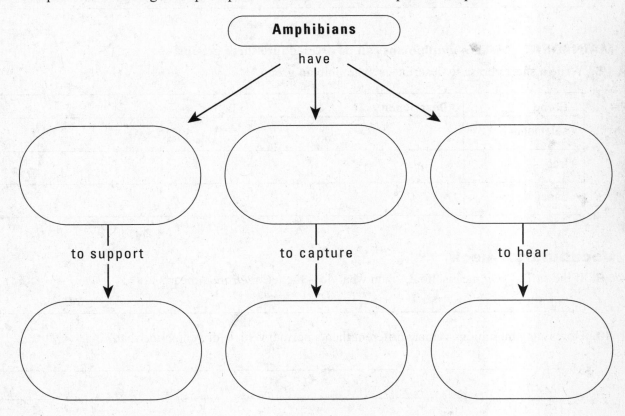

4. What are the different methods amphibians use to breathe?

_____

_____

MAIN IDEA: Amphibians return to the water to reproduce.

5. Why can't amphibians travel too far away from a source of water?

_____

6. List three strategies used by amphibians to keep their eggs moist.

_____

_____

7. Describe the changes a tadpole goes through during metamorphosis into an adult frog.

_____

_____

_____

MAIN IDEA: Modern amphibians can be divided into three groups.

8. Write a short phrase to describe each amphibian group.

Group	Description
salamander	
frog	
caecilian	

Vocabulary Check

9. If the suffix -pod means "foot," then what does the term *tetrapod* mean?

_____

10. How is an amphibious vehicle different than a normal vehicle driven on the road?

_____

_____

VERTEBRATES ON LAND
Study Guide

KEY CONCEPT
Reptiles, birds, and mammals are adapted for life on land.

<table>
<tr><td colspan="2">**VOCABULARY**</td></tr>
<tr><td>amniote</td><td>amniotic egg</td></tr>
<tr><td>keratin</td><td>placenta</td></tr>
</table>

MAIN IDEA: Amniotes can retain moisture.

1. What is an amniote?

_____

_____

2. List three examples of familiar animals that are amniotes. Are humans amniotes?
   Explain why or why not.

_____

_____

3. What is keratin used for?

_____

4. How do an amniote's kidneys and intestines help it to retain moisture?

_____

_____

MAIN IDEA: Amniotes do not need to return to water to reproduce.

5. How does the amniotic egg allow amniotes to live permanently on land?

_____

_____

6. What is the advantage for rattlesnakes to retain their eggs until they hatch?

_____

_____

7. What is the function of placenta?

_____

_____

Vocabulary Check

Choose a term from the box below that best fits each description.

amniote	amniotic egg	keratin	placenta

_____ **8.** I am a vertebrate that has a thin, tough, membranous sac that encloses the embryo or fetus during development.

_____ **9.** I am a protein that binds to lipids inside a skin cell, forming a water-repellent layer that keeps water from escaping.

_____ **10.** I am an almost completely waterproof container that keeps the embryo within from drying out.

_____ **11.** I am a membranous organ that develops in female mammals during pregnancy.

Be Creative

12. Draw a cartoon that illustrates the benefits of the amniotic egg.

SECTION
26.1

AMNIOTES
Study Guide

KEY CONCEPT
Reptiles, birds, and mammals are amniotes.

VOCABULARY	
pulmonary circuit	ectotherm
systemic circuit	endotherm

MAIN IDEA: Amniote embryos develop in a fluid-filled sac.

1. Why is it important that an amniotic egg shell is semi-permeable?

_____

2. Complete the following chart with a description of each type of membrane found within an amniotic egg. Use Figure 26.1 to help you.

Membrane	Description
allantois	
amnion	
chorion	
yolk sac	

3. Why was the development of the amniotic egg an important adaptation for amniotes?

_____

MAIN IDEA: Anatomy and circulation differ among amniotes.

4. What are three characteristics of a sprawling stance?

_____

5. What are three characteristics of an upright stance?

_____

6. What is the difference between the pulmonary circuit and the systemic circuit?

_____

_____

7. Use the Venn diagram below to list the differences between the circulatory system of a reptile and the circulatory system of a mammal.

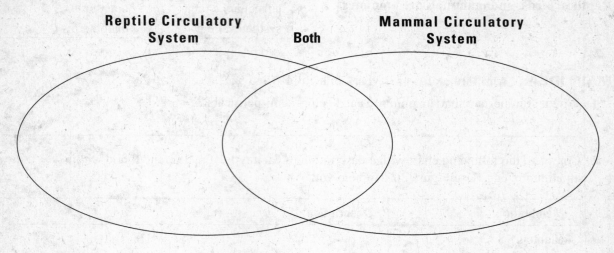

MAIN IDEA: **Amniotes can be ectothermic or endothermic.**

8. What is the difference between an ectotherm and an endotherm?

_____

_____

For each type of amniote, indicate whether it is an *ectotherm* or an *endotherm*.

_____   **9.** garter snake

_____   **10.** peregrine falcon

_____   **11.** your biology teacher

Vocabulary Check

12. What word in the term *systemic* can help you to remember the difference between the systemic circuit and the pulmonary circuit? Explain why.

_____

13. The prefix *endo-* means inner and the prefix *ecto-* means outer. Relate these two meanings to the definition of endotherm and ectotherm.

_____

SECTION
26.2

REPTILES
Study Guide

KEY CONCEPT
Reptiles were the first amniotes.

VOCABULARY	
reptile	viviparous
oviparous	

MAIN IDEA: Reptiles are a diverse group of amniotes.

1. What are three characteristics of a reptile?

   _____

2. What is the difference between oviparous and viviparous reptiles?

   _____

   _____

3. How do reptiles regulate their body temperature?

   _____

MAIN IDEA: Reptiles have been evolving for millions of years.

Choose the word from the box below that best fits each description.

anapsid	diapsid	synapsid

_____ **4.** Reptiles with one hole in each temporal region have this type of skull.

_____ **5.** Reptiles that have two holes in each temporal region, one above the other, have this type of skull.

_____ **6.** Reptiles that do not have any temporal holes have this type of skull.

7. When do dinosaurs first appear in the fossil record? When did all walking dinosaurs go extinct?

   _____

   _____

8. What were the first vertebrates to evolve powered flight?

   _____

MAIN IDEA: There are four modern group of reptiles.

9. Complete the following chart with details about the four modern groups of reptiles.

Group	Description	Example
turtles		
sphenodonts		
snakes and lizards		
crocodilians		

Vocabulary Check

10.

Word Part	Meaning
-parous	to give birth
ovi-	egg
vivi-	alive

Use the word parts in the table above to explain the difference between oviparous and viviparous reptiles.

_____

Be Creative

11. Draw a cartoon that illustrates the importance of a reptilian adaptation (for example, consider the function of a reptile's dry scales or plates, such as the hard shell of a turtle.)

SECTION 26.3 | BIRDS
Study Guide

KEY CONCEPT
Birds have many adaptations for flight.

MAIN IDEA: Birds evolved from theropod dinosaurs.

1. List the five anatomical characteristics shared by both birds and theropod dinosaurs.

   _____

   _____

2. What species is recognized as the oldest fossilized bird? How long ago did it live?

   _____

3. What is the difference between the "trees-down" hypothesis and the "ground-up" hypothesis for the origin of flight in birds?

   _____

   _____

MAIN IDEA: A bird's body is specialized for flight.

4. In the box below, draw an airfoil. Next to your picture, write a description of how the curved shape of a bird's wings helps it to fly.

   _____

   _____

   _____

   _____

   _____

5. Complete the table below with details about the specialized adaptations of a bird's body that allow it to fly.

Adaptation	How It Helps with Flight
wing shape	
chest muscles	
air sacs	
hollow bones	
reproductive organs	

MAIN IDEA: **Birds have spread to many ecological niches.**

6. List three ways in which birds have adapted to different habitats and methods of feeding.

_____

_____

Vocabulary Check

7. What is an air sac?

_____

8. How does a bird's sternum compare to yours? What is another name for it?

_____

_____

SECTION
26.4

MAMMALS
Study Guide

KEY CONCEPT
Evolutionary adaptations allowed mammals to succeed
dinosaurs as a dominant terrestrial vertebrate.

VOCABULARY	
mammal	marsupial
mammary gland	eutherian
monotreme	

MAIN IDEA: All mammals share several common characteristics.

1. What is a mammal?

   _____

2. List the four characteristics shared by all mammals.

   _____

3. What important adaptation gives mammals a distinct advantage over reptiles?

   _____

4. What is hair made out of and what is its function?

   _____

5. What are mammary glands?

   _____

6. What important nutrients does milk provide to a newborn?

   _____

Complete the following process diagram with details about how a mammal detects sound.

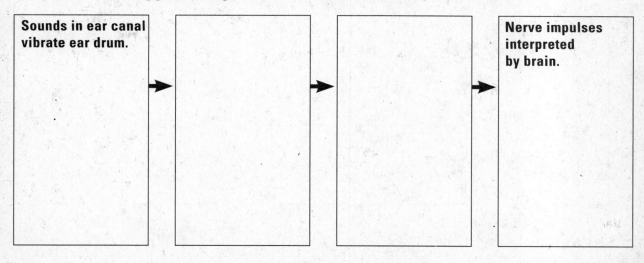

| Sounds in ear canal vibrate ear drum. | | | Nerve impulses interpreted by brain. |

7. How is a mammal able to chew and breathe at the same time?

_____

MAIN IDEA: **Modern mammals are divided into three main groups.**

8. Complete the following chart with details about the three main groups of modern mammals.

Group	Description	Example
monotremes		
marsupials		
eutherian mammals		

Vocabulary Check

9. The word *marsupial* comes from the Greek word *marsuppos*, which means "purse." Draw a picture of this word origin to help you remember the meaning of marsupial.

SECTION 27.1

ADAPTIVE VALUE OF BEHAVIOR

Study Guide

KEY CONCEPT
Behavior lets organisms respond rapidly and adaptively to their environment.

VOCABULARY		
stimulus	taxis	biological clock
kinesis	circadian rhythm	

MAIN IDEA: Behavioral responses to stimuli may be adaptive.

Choose a term or terms from the word box below to complete the following sentences.

behavior	external	stimulus
body	internal	surroundings

1. A _____ is a type of information that can make an organism change

   its _____.

2. _____ stimuli tell an animal what is occurring in its own

   _____.

3. _____ stimuli give an animal information about its _____.

Complete the cause-and-effect diagram to explain how a stimulus results in a behavior.

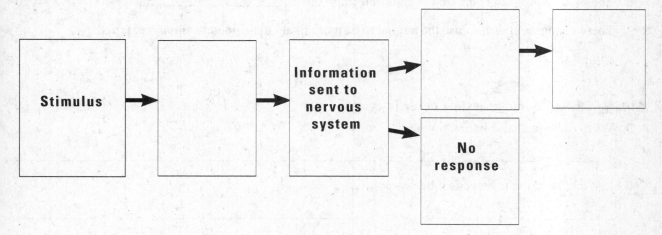

Stimulus → [ ] → Information sent to nervous system → [ ] → [ ]

No response

4. Homeostasis refers to the maintenance of constant internal conditions. How might an animal's behavior help to maintain homeostasis?

_____

5. What is the difference between kinesis and taxis?

_____

_____

MAIN IDEA: **Internal and external stimuli usually interact to trigger specific behaviors.**

Choose a term or terms from the word box below to complete the following sentences.

external	internal	hormones	physiological

6. Some behaviors can be triggered by a single stimulus, but most behaviors occur in response to a variety of _____ and _____ stimuli.

7. An external stimulus, such as a change in day length, might cause an animal to secrete specific _____.

8. These hormones act as internal signals that cause other _____ changes. These changes, in turn, cause the animal to be more likely to respond to another external stimulus.

MAIN IDEA: **Some behaviors occur in cycles.**

9. What is a circadian rhythm?

_____

10. List and describe two cyclical behaviors.

_____

_____

Vocabulary Check

11. The word *circadian* comes from a Latin word that means "circle." Explain the connection between these two words.

_____

**SECTION
27.2** | INSTINCT AND LEARNING
Study Guide

KEY CONCEPT

Both genes and environment affect an animal's behavior.

VOCABULARY		
instinct	habituation	classical conditioning
innate	imprinting	operant conditioning
releaser	imitation	

MAIN IDEA: **Innate behaviors are triggered by specific internal and external stimuli.**

1. What are two characteristics of instinctive behavior?

_____

2. Why are innate behaviors important for a newborn?

_____

_____

3. Consider the "nature versus nurture" debate. What factors influence innate behaviors?

_____

_____

MAIN IDEA: **Many behaviors have both innate and learned components.**

Choose the correct term from the box below that best fits each description.

habituation	imprinting	imitation

_____   **4.** rapid and irreversible learning process that only occurs during a short time in an animal's life

_____   **5.** a type of learning in which animals learn by observing the behavior of other animals

_____   **6.** a type of learning in which an animal learns to ignore a repeated stimulus

Section 27.2 STUDY GUIDE CONTINUED

MAIN IDEA: Learning is adaptive.

7. What is associative learning?

_____

_____

8. Complete the following concept map with details about classical and operant conditioning.

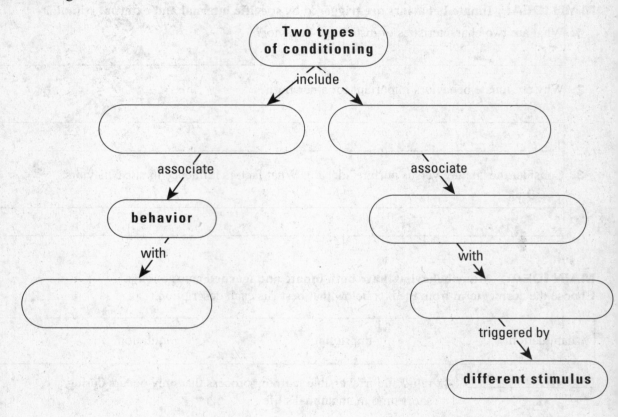

Vocabulary Check

9. What is a releaser?

_____

_____

10. Use your knowledge of the words "habit," "imitate," and "imprint" to write definitions for the vocabulary terms *habituation*, *imitation*, and *imprinting*.

_____

_____

_____

**SECTION
27.3** | EVOLUTION OF BEHAVIOR
Study Guide

KEY CONCEPT
Every beneficial behavior has costs and benefits.

VOCABULARY	
survivorship	optimal foraging
territoriality	

MAIN IDEA: **Even beneficial behaviors have associated costs.**

1. What are the two most important benefits of behavior?

_____

_____

2. Complete the following table with information about the three types of behavioral costs.

Cost of Behavior	Description

MAIN IDEA: **Animals perform behaviors that outweigh their costs.**

3. What is territoriality?

_____

4. What are the costs and benefits of territorial behavior?

_____

_____

5. What are the costs and benefits of foraging?

_____

_____

CHAPTER 27
Animal Behavior

6. What is the theory of optimal foraging?

_____

_____

Vocabulary Check

7. Use your knowledge of the words "survive" and "territory" to write definitions for the vocabulary words *survivorship* and *territoriality*.

_____

_____

Be Creative

8. In the box below, draw a cartoon that illustrates the costs and benefits of either territoriality or optimal foraging.

SECTION
27.4

SOCIAL BEHAVIOR
Study Guide

KEY CONCEPT

Social behaviors enhance the benefits
of living in a group.

VOCABULARY		
pheromone	inclusive fitness	eusocial
altruism	kin selection	

MAIN IDEA: Living in groups also has benefits and costs.

1. Complete the following table with three costs and three benefits of living in a group.

Benefits	Costs
(1)	(1)
(2)	(2)
(3)	(3)

MAIN IDEA: Social behaviors are interactions between members of the same or different species.

2. Describe the four main types of communication signals.

Communication Signal	Description
visual	
sound	
touch	
chemical	

3. What are courtship displays?

_____

_____

4. What do scientists think might be the evolutionary function of a courtship display?

_____

_____

Section 27.4 STUDY GUIDE CONTINUED·

5. Explain what defensive behaviors are and give an example.

_____

_____

MAIN IDEA: **Some behaviors benefit other group members at a cost to the individual performing them.**

Choose the correct term from the box below that best fits each description.

altruism inclusive fitness reciprocity cooperation kin selection

_____ **6.** behavior in which individuals help other group members so they will be helped in return

_____ **7.** the total number of genes an animal and its relatives contribute to the next generation

_____ **8.** behavior that helps both individuals

_____ **9.** type of natural selection acting on alleles that favor the survival of close relatives

_____ **10.** type of behavior in which an animal risks its life to help other group members

MAIN IDEA: **Eusocial behavior is an example of extreme altruism.**

11. List three characteristics of a eusocial species.

_____

_____

12. What is meant by the term *haplodiploid*?

_____

Vocabulary Check

13. What is a pheromone?

_____

14. Give an example of an altruistic behavior that might be performed by a human.

_____

SECTION 27.5

ANIMAL COGNITION
Study Guide

KEY CONCEPT
Some animals other than humans exhibit behaviors requiring complex cognitive abilities.

VOCABULARY	
cognition	cultural behavior
insight	

MAIN IDEA: Animal intelligence is difficult to define.

1. What are the characteristics of cognitive behavior?

_____

_____

2. Why is it easier to measure an animal's cognitive abilities rather than its level of intelligence?

_____

_____

MAIN IDEA: Some animals can solve problems.

3. What is insight?

_____

_____

4. What does tool use suggest about an animal's cognitive abilities?

_____

_____

MAIN IDEA: Cognitive ability may provide an adaptive advantage for living in social groups.

5. What are two characteristics of animals considered to be most "intelligent"?

_____

_____

6. What is cultural behavior?

_____

_____

Section 27.5 STUDY GUIDE CONTINUED

Vocabulary Check

7. What is cognition?

_____

_____

8. What does it mean to solve a problem by using insight? What is the opposite of using insight?

_____

_____

Be Creative

9. Draw a four-panel cartoon that illustrates how an animal might use a tool to solve a problem.

SECTION 28.1 | LEVELS OF ORGANIZATION
Study Guide

KEY CONCEPT
The human body has five levels of organization.

VOCABULARY	
determination	organ
differentiation	organ system
tissue	

MAIN IDEA: Specialized cells develop from a single zygote.
Fill in the main idea and supporting information for cell development.

1. Stem cells:

2. Determination

3. Differentiation

4. What are the characteristics of stem cells?

_____

_____

5. Look at Figure 28.2. Describe some of the shapes and structures that the cells in this figure acquired during differentiation.

_____

_____

_____

6. Give two examples of how cell structures relate to cell functions.

_____

_____

_____

CHAPTER 28
Human Systems and Homeostasis

MAIN IDEA: Specialized cells function together in tissues, organs, organ systems, and the whole organism.

7. Write a description of each level of organization and draw a sketch to help you remember it.

Level of Organization	Description	Sketch

Vocabulary Check

8. There is an easy way to remember the difference between *determination* and *differentiation*. Look at the first part of each word. Explain how these word parts can help you remember the meaning of each term.

_____

_____

SECTION
28.2

MECHANISMS OF HOMEOSTASIS
Study Guide

KEY CONCEPT

Homeostasis is the regulation and maintenance of the internal environment.

VOCABULARY	
homeostasis	negative feedback
feedback	positive feedback

MAIN IDEA: **Conditions within the body must remain within a narrow range.**

1. Give two reasons why it is so important that the internal environment of the body remains stable.

_____

_____

_____

2. Homeostasis is maintained by control systems. Fill in the name and function of the parts of the control system in the cycle diagram below.

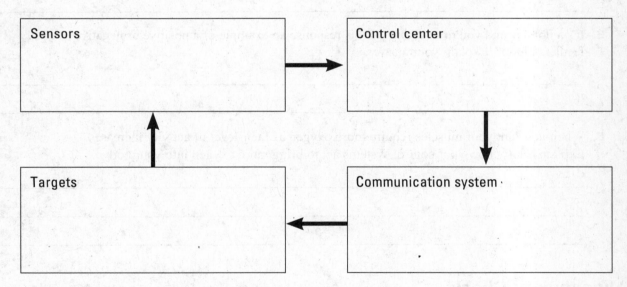

3. What might happen if a target organ cannot respond?

_____

_____

_____

CHAPTER 28
Human Systems and Homeostasis

Section 28.2 STUDY GUIDE CONTINUED

MAIN IDEA: Negative feedback loops are necessary for homeostasis.

4. Study the following line drawings. Which of the following diagrams represents negative feedback and which represents positive feedback? Explain your answer.

A.
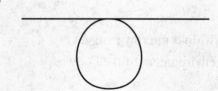

B.
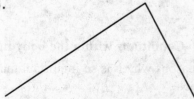

_____

_____

5. It's a hot day and you're sweating. Is this response an example of a positive or negative feedback loop? Explain your answer.

_____

_____

6. When you run, your muscles require more oxygen as their level of activity increases. Explain briefly how your control systems act to bring more oxygen into your body.

_____

_____

_____

Vocabulary Check

7. What is the difference between positive and negative feedback loops?

_____

_____

8. Think of an analogy that would illustrate the process of feedback for someone who does not know what the word means.

_____

SECTION 28.3 | INTERACTIONS AMONG SYSTEMS
Study Guide

KEY CONCEPT
Systems interact to maintain homeostasis.

VOCABULARY
thermoregulation

MAIN IDEA: **Each organ affects other organ systems.**

1. The organs in the body work together like members of a pit crew servicing a race car. What other analogies can you think of to illustrate organ systems working together?

_____

_____

_____

2. Fill in the table below to explain what each organ does to help produce vitamin D in your body.

Organ	Function
Skin	
Liver	
Kidneys	

3. What role does the hypothalamus play to help regulate body temperature?

_____

_____

_____

MAIN IDEA: **A disruption of homeostasis can be harmful.**

4. List three reasons why homeostasis in the body might be disrupted.

_____

_____

Section 28.3 STUDY GUIDE CONTINUED

5. Why is a long-term disruption of homeostasis usually more serious than a short-term disruption?

_____

_____

Fill in the concept map to help you remember what you know about long-term and short-term disruption of homeostasis.

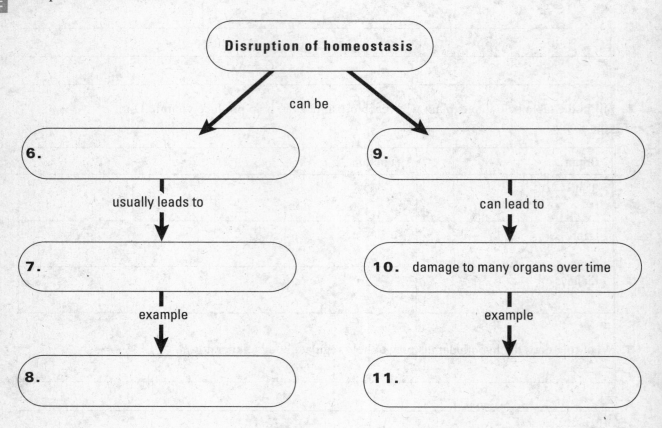

Vocabulary Check

11. Think of a diagram that might illustrate the term *thermoregulation* for someone unfamiliar with the word. Use the space below to sketch your diagram.

SECTION
29.1

HOW ORGAN SYSTEMS COMMUNICATE
Study Guide

KEY CONCEPT

The nervous system and the endocrine system provide the means by which organ systems communicate.

VOCABULARY	
nervous system	central nervous system (CNS)
endocrine system	peripheral nervous system (PNS)
stimulus	

MAIN IDEA: The body's communication systems help maintain homeostasis.

1. What is homeostasis?

_____

2. How do communication systems allow the body to maintain homeostasis?

_____

You work for a new kind of textbook company, one whose textbooks are actually comic books! Using the boxes provided, create a comic strip that shows an example of how a stimulus causes the human body to respond. (If you can't come up with an example, use the one in the text that describes how your eyes respond to bright sunlight.)

MAIN IDEA: **The nervous and endocrine systems have different methods and rates of communication.**

Fill out the Y diagram below. In the top left, write the characteristics of the nervous system. In the top right, write the characteristics of the endocrine system. At the bottom, write the characteristics the two systems have in common. Then, lightly cross out those characteristics at the top.

Nervous system

_____

_____

_____

_____

Endocrine system

_____

_____

_____

_____

Both

_____

_____

_____

_____

Vocabulary Check

Use the vocabulary terms from this section to complete the following sentences.

3. When you stand on a street corner, you jump when you hear a nearby truck honk its

horn. In this example, the honking horn is the _____ .

4. The _____ sends chemical signals through the bloodstream.

5. When your brain wants to make your legs move so that you can run, the

_____ carries the message from your spinal cord to your leg

muscles.

6. Your _____ is the communication system that sends its signals

through a highly connected network of specialized cells and tissues.

SECTION
29.2 | NEURONS
Study Guide

KEY CONCEPT
The nervous system is composed of highly specialized cells.

VOCABULARY	
neuron	action potential
dendrite	synapse
axon	terminal
resting potential	neurotransmitter
sodium-potassium pump	

MAIN IDEA: Neurons are highly specialized cells.

Use the concept map to organize your notes on neurons.

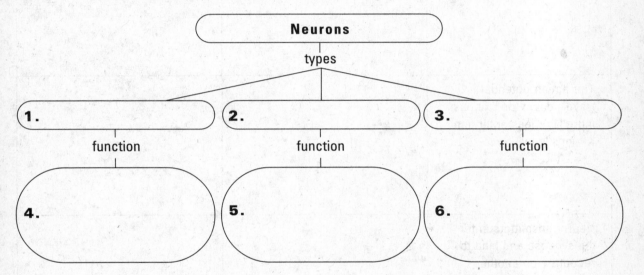

7. What is the difference between the function of an axon and a dendrite?

_____

_____

_____

MAIN IDEA: **Neurons receive and transmit signals.**

8. What is the role of the sodium-potassium pump?

_____

9. Draw a picture to match each of the captions in the table. In the third column, write additional details about what is happening in each of your drawings.

Caption	Drawing	Description
The neuron is stimulated and Na+ ions flow into the axon.		
The action potential travels down the axon as more Na+ ions enter and K+ ions leave.		
Neurotransmitters enter the synapse and bind to receptors on another neuron, stimulating Na+ ions to enter that cell.		

10. What happens after neurotransmitters bind to the other neuron's receptors?

_____

Vocabulary Check

_____ **11.** the molecule that transmits a signal from one neuron to another

_____ **12.** a gap between neurons

_____ **13.** end of an axon

_____ **14.** moving electrical impulse

SECTION
29.3
THE SENSES
Study Guide

KEY CONCEPT
The senses detect the internal and external environments.

VOCABULARY		
rod cell	cone cell	hair cell

MAIN IDEA: The senses help to maintain homeostasis.

1. What do you rely on your senses to do?

_____

2. Give an example of how your sensory organs work with your brain to help you to maintain homeostasis?

_____

_____

MAIN IDEA: The senses detect physical and chemical stimuli.

Use the chart below to organize your notes on the senses. For each of the senses shown in the first column, write the types of receptors that contribute to this sense. In the third column, write what kind of stimuli that the receptor detects. Include any additional notes or important details about that sense in the last column.

Sense	Receptor	Stimuli It Detects	Additional Notes
3. Vision			
4. Hearing			
5. Smell			
6. Taste			
7. Touch			

8. What part of the eye contains the receptors?

_____

9. Explain how sound waves interact with the structures of the middle ear and, eventually, generate impulses that cause hearing.

_____

_____

10. Before chemicals can be detected by the tongue or nose, what must happen to them?

_____

11. What types of receptors will be activated when you get a paper cut on your finger?

_____

Vocabulary Check

12. Fill in the chart below.

	Rod Cell	Cone Cell	Hair Cell
What does it do?			
Where is it found?			

Activity

Pick one of the five senses, and design a bumper sticker that has a catchy slogan that explains a little bit about the function of the sense you picked.

SECTION 29.4

CENTRAL AND PERIPHERAL NERVOUS SYSTEMS
Study Guide

KEY CONCEPT

The central nervous system interprets information, and the peripheral nervous system gathers and transmits information.

VOCABULARY		
cerebrum	brain stem	autonomic nervous system
cerebral cortex	reflex arc	sympathetic nervous system
cerebellum	somatic nervous system	parasympathetic nervous system

MAIN IDEA: The nervous system's two parts work together.

1. What organs make up the central nervous system?

_____

2. What types of neurons make up the peripheral nervous system?

_____

On the first page of this section, you read about how the nerves, brain, and spinal cord work together to produce a response. Use the cause-and-effect diagram below to trace how the nervous system produces a response to a stimulus.

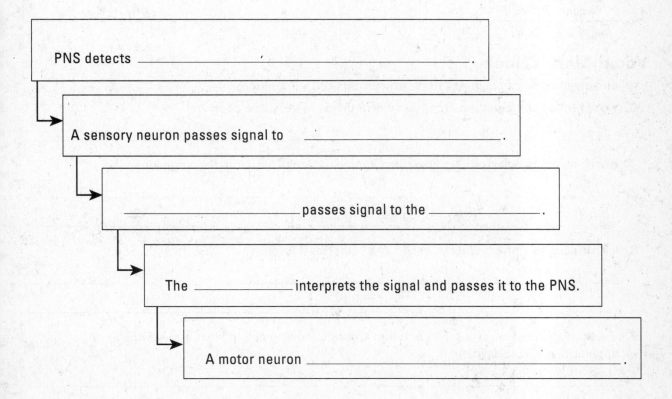

PNS detects _____.

A sensory neuron passes signal to _____.

_____ passes signal to the _____.

The _____ interprets the signal and passes it to the PNS.

A motor neuron _____.

Section 29.4 STUDY GUIDE CONTINUED

MAIN IDEA: The CNS processes information.

3. What is the role of the cerebrum?

_____

4. What are the three main structures of the brain?

_____

MAIN IDEA: The PNS links the CNS to the muscles and other organs.

5. Use the chart to take notes on the peripheral nervous system.

Division of the PNS	Voluntary or Involuntary?	Examples of Tissues It Stimulates
somatic nervous system		
autonomic nervous system		
sympathetic nervous system		
parasympathetic nervous system		

Vocabulary Check

Explain how the clue can help you to remember the word's definition.

6. **word:** reflex arc; **clue:** An *arc* is movement that is in the shape of an arch.

_____

7. **word:** autonomic nervous system; **clue:** *Autonomic* looks similar to the word *automatic*.

_____

_____

8. **word:** cerebral cortex; **clue:** A *cortex* is an outermost layer.

_____

_____

9. **word:** sympathetic nervous system; **clue:** Consider how something that is *sympathetic* might affect homeostasis.

_____

SECTION
29.5 | BRAIN FUNCTION AND CHEMISTRY
Study Guide

KEY CONCEPT
Scientists study the functions and chemistry of the brain.

VOCABULARY		
addiction	tolerance	stimulant
desensitization	sensitization	depressant

MAIN IDEA: New techniques improve our understanding of the brain.

Organize your notes on technologies used to study the brain in this three-column chart.

Imaging Technology	What scans the brain?	What is shown in the image?
1. Computerized tomography (CT)	x-rays	
2.		activity in the brain
3.		

MAIN IDEA: Changes in brain chemistry can cause illness.

Write the word(s) that completes each sentence.

4. Chemicals called _____ allow neurons in the brain to

communicate with one another.

5. The _____ of neurotransmitter in an area of the brain affects

how stimulated that area will be.

6. The PET scans in Figure 29.15 show what areas of the brain are

_____.

7. Depression and Alzheimer's disease are examples of mental illness linked to

_____ in the brain.

8. Drugs that treat mental illness affect the _____ that neurons

generate.

Section 29.5 STUDY GUIDE CONTINUED

MAIN IDEA: Drugs alter brain chemistry.

9. What are some of the effects drugs can have on a person's behavior?

_____

10. What are the two ways that drugs affect the brain's chemistry?

_____

11. What in the brain do drugs have an effect on?

_____

12. How does the brain's ability to adapt when it experiences long periods of too much or too little neurotransmitter help it maintain homeostasis?

_____

13. How does a stimulant affect brain function?

_____

14. How does a depressant affect brain function?

_____

Vocabulary Check

For each of the word pairs, write a sentence or two that explains how the two terms are different from one another.

15. Addiction, Tolerance

_____

_____

_____

16. Desensitization, Sensitization

_____

_____

_____

17. Stimulant, Depressant

_____

_____

_____

CHAPTER 29
Nervous and Endocrine Systems

SECTION 29.6 THE ENDOCRINE SYSTEM AND HORMONES
Study Guide

KEY CONCEPT
The endocrine system produces hormones that affect growth, development, and homeostasis.

<table>
<tr><td colspan="3">VOCABULARY</td></tr>
<tr><td>hormone</td><td>hypothalamus</td><td>releasing hormone</td></tr>
<tr><td>gland</td><td>pituitary gland</td><td></td></tr>
</table>

MAIN IDEA: Hormones influence a cell's activities by entering the cell or binding to its membrane.

1. How do hormones get from the gland that produced them to the cells they will affect?

_____

2. What determines whether or not a hormone will affect a cell?

_____

3. How are steroid hormones different from nonsteroid hormones?

_____

MAIN IDEA: Endocrine glands secrete hormones that act throughout the body.
Use the text and Figure 29.20 to fill in the chart.

Gland	Location	Secretes Hormones that Control
4. hypothalamus		
5.	brain	
6.		metabolism, growth, and development
7.	chest	
8.		blood pressure, breathing rate, fight-or-flight response
9.		digestion and glucose metabolism
10. gonads	pelvis	

MAIN IDEA: The hypothalamus interacts with the nervous system and endocrine system.

Draw the diagram of a hormone feedback loop on p. 900, and answer the following questions.

11. Which of the hormones in your diagram are releasing hormones?

_____

_____

12. What stimulates the hypothalamus to stop producing TRH?

_____

_____

13. Explain why the thyroid gland will stop producing thyroxine when the body warms.

_____

_____

_____

MAIN IDEA: Hormonal imbalances can cause severe illness.

14. How do hormone imbalances cause illness in many different body systems?

_____

Vocabulary Check

For each term, write a clue that helps you to remember the word's definition.

15. Hormone

_____

16. Pituitary gland

_____

17. Hypothalamus

_____

SECTION
30.1 | RESPIRATORY AND CIRCULATORY FUNCTIONS
Study Guide

KEY CONCEPT

The respiratory and circulatory systems bring oxygen and nutrients to the cells.

VOCABULARY		
circulatory system	alveoli	vein
respiratory system	diaphragm	capillary
trachea	heart	
lung	artery	

MAIN IDEA: The respiratory and circulatory systems work together to maintain homeostasis.

Fill in the Q and A chart below about the circulatory and respiratory systems.

Questions	Answers
1. What are the main functions of the circulatory system?	
2. What are the main functions of the respiratory system?	

MAIN IDEA: The respiratory system moves gases into and out of the blood.

3. What pathway does air follow after it enters the nose and mouth?

_____

_____

4. Explain why so much surface area is needed in the lungs.

_____

5. As shown in Figure 30.2, when you inhale, the muscles of the rib cage contract, expanding the rib cage. The diaphragm flattens and moves downward, and air flows into the lungs. What happens when you exhale?

_____

Section 30.1 STUDY GUIDE CONTINUED

MAIN IDEA: **The circulatory system moves blood to all parts of the body.**

6. Fill in the chart to help you remember the parts of the circulatory system and their functions.

Part	Function
heart	
arteries	
veins	
capillaries	

7. How do the heart and blood vessels maintain a stable body temperature in hot and cold weather?

_____

_____

Vocabulary Check

8. The word *diaphragm* is based on the Latin word *diaphragma*, which means "midriff." How does this term relate to the meaning of *diaphragm*?

_____

_____

9. The trachea, bronchi, and bronchioles have been compared to the trunk, branches, and twigs of a tree. What other analogy can you think of to describe these structures?

_____

_____

_____

SECTION
30.2
RESPIRATION AND GAS EXCHANGE
Study Guide

KEY CONCEPT
The respiratory system exchanges oxygen and carbon dioxide.

VOCABULARY	
red blood cell	emphysema
hemoglobin	asthma

MAIN IDEA: **Gas exchange occurs in the alveoli of the lungs.**

1. What are the three principles of gas exchange?

_____

_____

2. What is the advantage of having so many clusters of alveoli in the lungs?

_____

Fill in diagram A about oxygen diffusion and diagram B about carbon dioxide diffusion. Add arrows to show the direction in which the gases move.

A

Alveolus	**Capillary and alveolus walls**	**Capillary**
O_2 concentrations are higher than in the capillary.		

B

Alveolus	**Capillary and alveolus walls**	**Capillary**
		CO_2 and water vapor concentrations are higher than in alveolus.

Section 30.2 STUDY GUIDE CONTINUED

3. What is the function of hemoglobin in red blood cells?

_____

_____

_____

4. When CO_2 levels in the blood increase, how does the nervous system respond?

_____

_____

MAIN IDEA: **Respiratory diseases interfere with gas exchange.**

5. In the chart below, summarize how each activity or disease affects the lungs' ability to exchange gases.

Activity or Disease	Effect on Lungs
smoking	
emphysema	
asthma	
cystic fibrosis	

Vocabulary Check

6. *Asthma* comes from the Greek word *asthma*, which means "to pant." How does this meaning relate to the definition of *asthma*?

_____

_____

7. What is the definition of *hemoglobin*? Why does it give blood its reddish color?

_____

_____

SECTION
30.3 | THE HEART AND CIRCULATION
Study Guide

KEY CONCEPT

The heart is a muscular pump that
moves the blood through two pathways.

VOCABULARY	
atrium	pacemaker
ventricle	pulmonary circulation
valve	systemic circulation

MAIN IDEA: The tissues and structures of the heart make it an efficient pump.
Fill in the pattern notes with the main chambers and valves of the heart. Use Figure 30.7 to
help you.

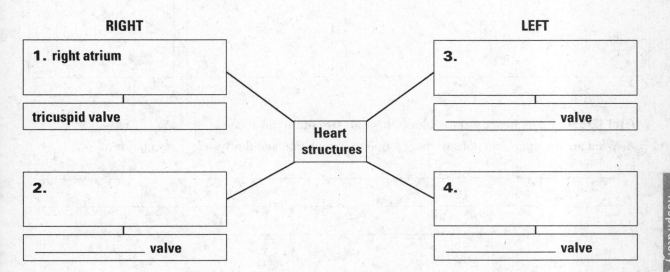

RIGHT   LEFT

1. right atrium   3.

tricuspid valve   _____ valve

Heart structures

2.   4.

_____ valve   _____ valve

5. Explain what makes the heart such an efficient, self-regulating pump.

_____

_____

_____

6. After the SA node stimulates the atria to contract, what happens next in the heartbeat
cycle?

_____

_____

CHAPTER 30
Respiratory and Circulatory

Section 30.3 STUDY GUIDE CONTINUED

Fill in the process diagram below to summarize the blood flow in the heart.

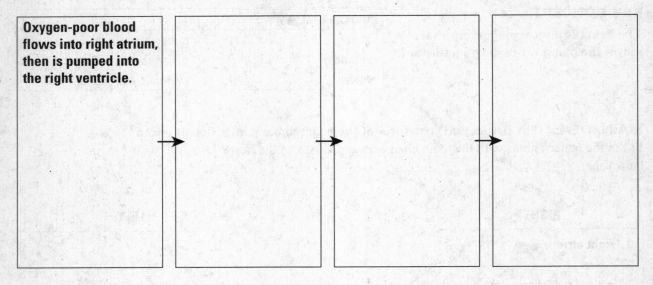

| Oxygen-poor blood flows into right atrium, then is pumped into the right ventricle. | → | | → | | → | |

MAIN IDEA: **The heart pumps blood through two main pathways.**

7. What are the main functions of the pulmonary circulation and the systemic circulation?

_____

_____

_____

Vocabulary Check

8. An *atrium* in a building is the first room or area that people enter before going into the rest of the building. How does this meaning relate to the location and function of an atrium in the heart?

_____

9. *Systemic* means "related to a an entire system," while *pulmonary* is based on the Latin *pulmo*, which means "lung." Make up a table or draw a diagram using these clues to help you remember the difference between *pulmonary* and *systemic* circulations.

SECTION
30.4

BLOOD VESSELS AND TRANSPORT
Study Guide

KEY CONCEPT
The circulatory system transports materials throughout the body.

VOCABULARY

blood pressure	diastolic pressure
systolic pressure	

MAIN IDEA: **Arteries, veins, and capillaries transport blood to all parts of the body.**

Fill in the Y diagram to summarize what you know about the differences and similarities between arteries and veins.

Arteries
- carry oxygen-rich blood away from heart
  _____
  _____
  _____

Veins
- carry oxygen-poor blood back to heart
  _____
  _____
  _____

Both
- carry blood throughout entire body
  _____
  _____
  _____
  _____
  _____

1. Describe how capillaries differ from arteries and veins.

_____

_____

_____

2. When a doctor takes your blood pressure, what is he or she measuring?

_____

_____

CHAPTER 30
Respiratory and Circulatory

Section 30.4 STUDY GUIDE CONTINUED

3. What is the difference between systolic pressure and diastolic pressure?

_____

_____

_____

4. Why is hypertension, or high blood pressure, a serious health risk?

_____

MAIN IDEA: Lifestyle plays a key role in circulatory diseases.

Complete the following concept web to show how lifestyle choices can affect circulatory health.

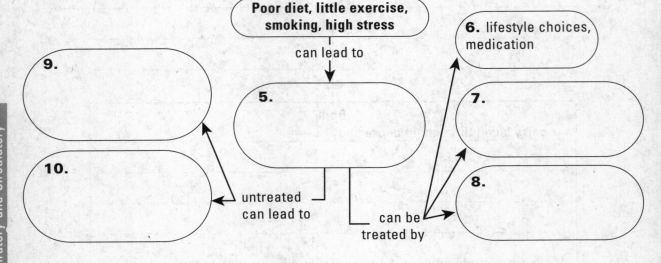

Vocabulary Check

11. *Systolic* is based on the Greek word *sustellein*, which means "to contract." *Diastolic* is based on the Greek word *diastellein*, which means "to expand." How can the meaning of these Greek words help you remember the difference between systolic and diastolic pressure?

_____

_____

SECTION 30.5 | BLOOD
Study Guide

KEY CONCEPT
Blood is a complex tissue that transports materials.

VOCABULARY		
platelet	ABO blood group	white blood cells
plasma	Rh factor	

MAIN IDEA: **Blood is composed mainly of cells, cell fragments, and plasma.**

Complete the following concept web to help you remember the components in blood.

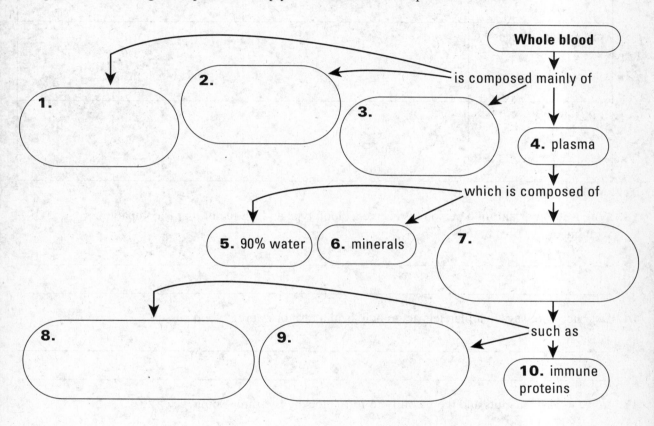

Whole blood

is composed mainly of

1.

2.

3.

4. plasma

which is composed of

5. 90% water

6. minerals

7.

8.

9.

such as

10. immune proteins

11. Summarize how plasma proteins and the water in plasma help to maintain homeostasis in the body.

_____

_____

_____

_____

MAIN IDEA: Platelets and different types of cells have different functions.

12. Complete the chart below to describe the structures and functions of blood cells and platelets.

Blood Component	Structure	Functions
Red blood cells		
White blood cells		
Platelets		

13. Why is it important for a person to receive a blood type and Rh factor that is compatible with his or her own blood?

_____

_____

14. Describe two ways that platelets act to help heal a torn or injured blood vessel.

_____

_____

15. In what way can clots and the inability to form clots be life-threatening?

_____

Vocabulary Check

16. What does the term *ABO blood group* stand for?

_____

17. To keep from getting *plasma* and *platelet* confused, remember that the suffix *-let* means "small." *Platelet* is a small part of a cell. Draw and label a sketch of a platelet and plasma to help you remember the difference between these two terms.

CHAPTER 30
Respiratory and Circulatory

SECTION 30.6

LYMPHATIC SYSTEM
Study Guide

KEY CONCEPT
The lymphatic system provides another type of circulation in the body.

VOCABULARY	
lymphatic system	node
lymph	lymphocyte

MAIN IDEA: Lymph is collected from tissues and returned to the circulatory system.

1. What are the main functions of the lymphatic system?

   _____

   _____

2. The lymphatic system, unlike the circulatory system, has no pump that moves the fluid. What keeps lymph moving in the lymph vessels?

   _____

   _____

Fill in the cycle diagram below that traces the pathway of lymphatic circulation.

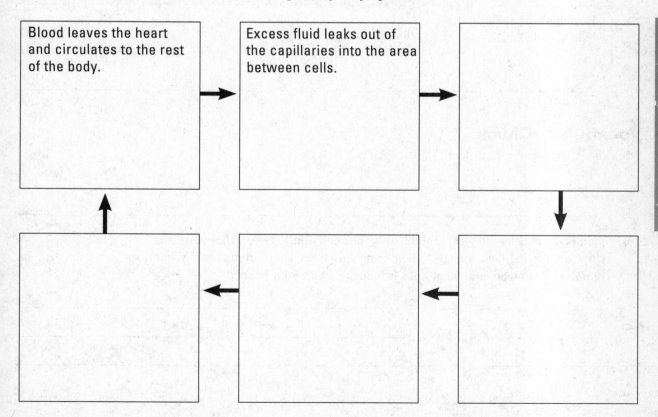

Blood leaves the heart and circulates to the rest of the body. → Excess fluid leaks out of the capillaries into the area between cells. →

CHAPTER 30
Respiratory and Circulatory

3. Suppose the lymphatic system was unable to function in one area of the body. What would you expect to happen in that area?

_____

_____

MAIN IDEA: **The lymphatic system is a major part of the immune system.**

4. Complete the question and answer note taking chart below.

Question	Answer
How do the tonsils help fight disease?	
What role does the thymus play in the immune system?	
How does the spleen help fight disease?	

Vocabulary Check

5. The suffix -*cyte* means "cell." What then is a *lymphocyte?*

_____

_____

6. The doctor checks the lymph nodes in your neck and tells you that you have lymphadenitis. *Adeno-* means "gland" and -*itis* means "inflammation." What does *lymphadenitis* mean, and what does it indicate about your health?

_____

_____

_____

PATHOGENS AND HUMAN ILLNESS
Study Guide

KEY CONCEPT
Germs cause many diseases in humans.

VOCABULARY		
germ theory	pathogen	vector

MAIN IDEA: Germ theory states that microscopic particles cause certain diseases.
Use the concept map below to take notes on early research about infectious diseases.

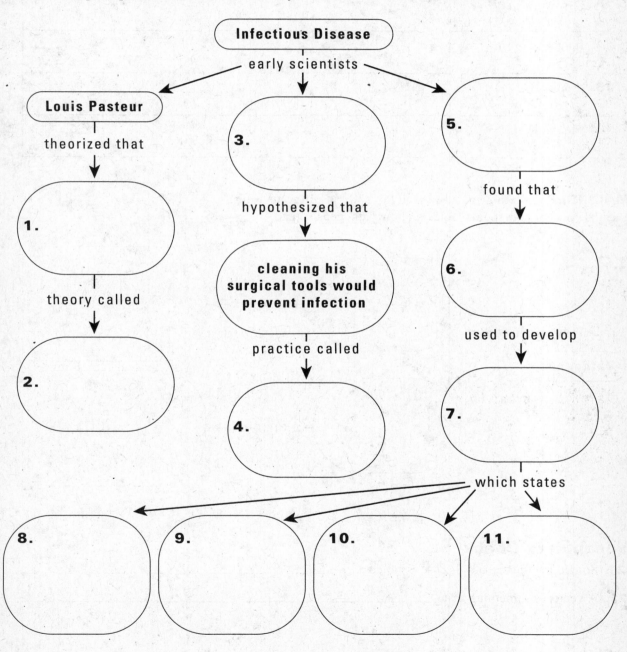

CHAPTER 31
Immune System and Disease

MAIN IDEA: There are different types of pathogens.

Fill in the chart to take notes on the different types of pathogens.

Pathogen	Causes Disease By:
12. bacteria	
13. viruses	
14. fungi	
15. protozoa	
16. parasites	

MAIN IDEA: Pathogens can enter the body in different ways.

Use the concept map to take notes on how pathogens spread.

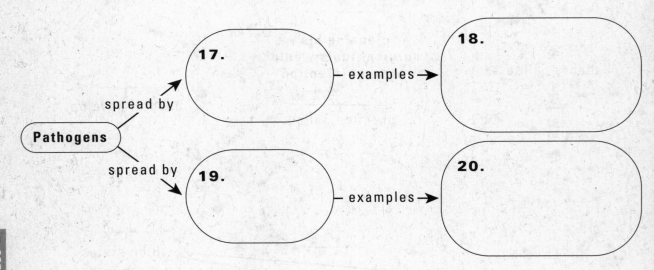

Vocabulary Check

21. Something that causes disease is called a _____

22. A vector is something that _____

SECTION
31.2 | IMMUNE SYSTEM
Study Guide

KEY CONCEPT
The immune system consists of organs, cells, and molecules that fight infections.

VOCABULARY		
immune system	B cell	passive immunity
phagocyte	antibody	active immunity
T cell	interferon	

MAIN IDEA: Many body systems protect you from pathogens.

1. What is the immune system?

_____

_____

2. For each, describe how it helps the immune system by protecting the body from pathogens.

Tissue or Body System	How It Protects the Body from Infection
skin	
mucus membrane	
circulatory system	

MAIN IDEA: Cells and proteins fight the body's infections.

3. How do your basophil cells react when a pathogen enters the body?

_____

_____

4. What are three ways that antibodies help fight infection?

_____

_____

Section 31.2 STUDY GUIDE CONTINUED

MAIN IDEA: Immunity prevents a person from getting sick from a pathogen.

Fill in the blanks in the concept map to take notes on the differences between active and passive immunity.

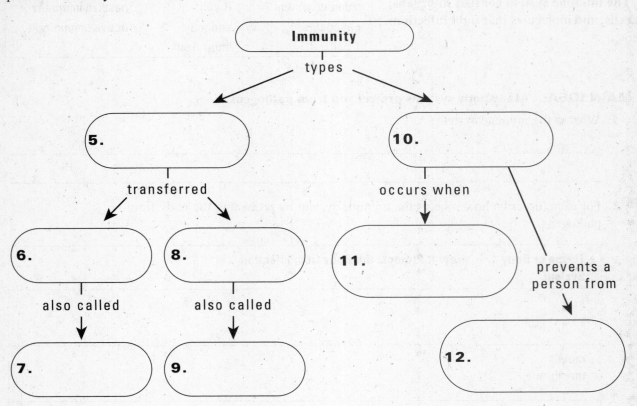

Vocabulary Check

13. Come up with a way to remember the difference between B cells and T cells.

_____

_____

14. The word *phagocyte* comes from two Greek words: *phago-* means "to eat" and *-cyte* means cell. How can this help you remember the definition of the word *phagocyte?*

_____

15. *Interferon* is similar to the word *interference*. How can this clue help you remember what *interferon* means?

_____

_____

IMMUNE RESPONSES
Study Guide

KEY CONCEPT
The immune system has many responses to pathogens and foreign cells.

VOCABULARY		
inflammation	memory cell	humoral immunity
antigen	cellular immunity	tissue rejection

MAIN IDEA: Many body systems work to produce nonspecific responses.

1. What is the difference between a specific immune response and a nonspecific immune response?

_____

_____

In the table, write the characteristics of each of the nonspecific immune responses. Then, in the third column, explain how this nonspecific response helps the immune system to fight off infections.

Nonspecific Response	Characteristics	How It Helps the Immune System
2. inflammation		
3. fever		

MAIN IDEA: Cells of the immune system produce specific responses.

4. How does the immune system know if a foreign particle has infected the body?

_____

_____

5. What is the role of memory cells in providing acquired immunity?

_____

_____

_____

Section 31.3 STUDY GUIDE CONTINUED

Using Figures 31.10 and 31.11, write the differences for each type of immunity on the right or left side of the Y diagram below. Then, write the similarities on the bottom of the Y.

Humoral Immunity   **Cellular Immunity**

_____   _____

_____   _____

_____   _____

_____   _____

_____

Both

_____

_____

_____

_____

_____

_____

MAIN IDEA: The immune system rejects foreign tissues.

6. Donors and recipients should have _____ differing antigens.

7. An organ recipient takes drugs that _____ the immune system.

Vocabulary Check

8. What do *memory cells* remember?

_____

9. How does the word *rejection* help you to remember what *tissue rejection* means?

_____

_____

10. The prefix *anti-* means "destroying" and, the suffix *-gen* means "something that produces or lives." How can this help you remember the definition for the word *antigen?*

_____

SECTION
31.4
IMMUNITY AND TECHNOLOGY
Study Guide

KEY CONCEPT

Living in a clean environment and building immunity helps to keep a person healthy.

VOCABULARY		
antiseptic	antibiotic resistance	vaccine

MAIN IDEA: Many methods are used to control pathogens.

Use the concept map to take notes on the different technologies that have been developed to destroy pathogens.

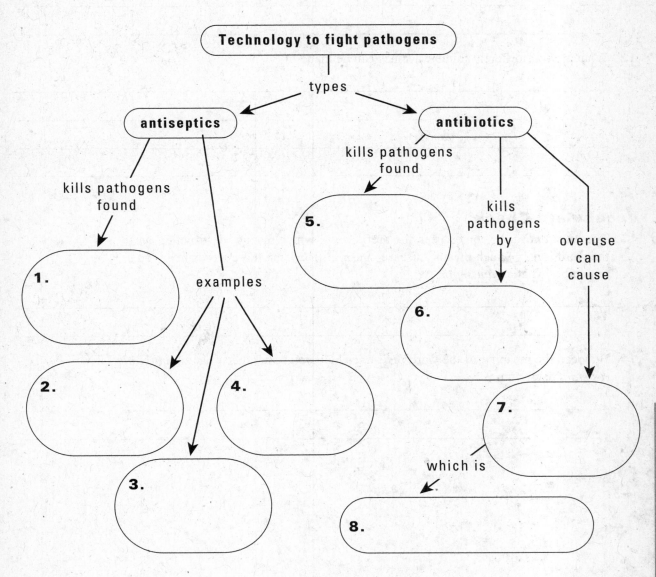

MAIN IDEA: Vaccines artificially produce acquired immunity.

9. What is a vaccine?

_____

10. What do vaccines do that allow the body to gain immunity without ever getting sick?

_____

11. Why does a person who has memory cells for a pathogen not get sick, while a person without memory cells for a pathogen will get sick?

_____

_____

12. What are four different things vaccines can be made of?

_____

_____

_____

_____

Vocabulary Check

13. The word *antiseptic* comes from the prefix *anti-,* which means "destroying," and the word *septic,* which means "disease-causing." How can these words help you to remember what an *antiseptic* is?

_____

_____

14. How can the meaning of the word *resistance* help you remember what an *antibiotic resistant* bacterium is?

_____

_____

OVERREACTIONS OF THE IMMUNE SYSTEM
Study Guide

KEY CONCEPT
An overactive immune system can make the body very unhealthy.

VOCABULARY		
allergy	allergen	anaphylaxis

MAIN IDEA: Allergies occur when the immune system responds to harmless antigens.

1. What triggers an allergic reaction?

_____

2. What do white blood cells do that causes an allergic reaction?

_____

3. Use the chart to take notes on the types of allergens.

Allergen Category	Symptoms of Allergic Reaction	Examples of Allergen
food allergen		
airborne allergen		
chemical allergen		

Section 31.5 STUDY GUIDE CONTINUED

MAIN IDEA: In autoimmune diseases, white blood cells attack the body's healthy cells.

4. What are two things that occur when a person has Type 1 diabetes?

_____

_____

_____

5. How do medications help people with autoimmune diseases?

_____

_____

_____

Vocabulary Check

6. The suffix *auto-* means "self." How can this help you to remember what an autoimmune disease is?

_____

_____

7. What is the difference between the word **allergy** and the word **allergen?**

_____

_____

8. What symptoms does a person have if they are experiencing anaphylaxis?

_____

_____

SECTION
31.6

DISEASES THAT WEAKEN THE IMMUNE SYSTEM
Study Guide

KEY CONCEPT

When the immune system is weakened, the body cannot fight off diseases.

VOCABULARY	
leukemia	human immunodeficiency virus (HIV)
opportunistic infection	acquired immune deficiency syndrome (AIDS)

MAIN IDEA: **Leukemia is characterized by abnormal white blood cells.**

Fill in the boxes of the flow chart to show how leukemia can lead to opportunistic diseases.

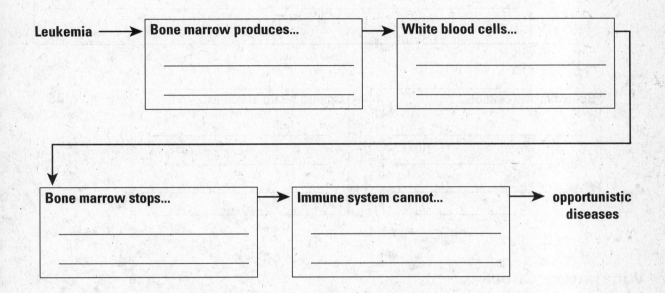

Leukemia → Bone marrow produces... → White blood cells... → Bone marrow stops... → Immune system cannot... → opportunistic diseases

MAIN IDEA: **HIV targets the immune system.**

1. What are three examples of the ways HIV can be passed from person to person?

_____

_____

_____

_____

Use the flow chart to explain how HIV infection leads to AIDS.

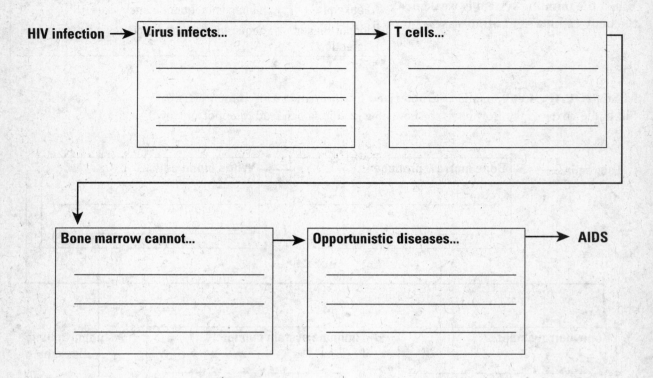

HIV infection →

Virus infects...

_____

_____

_____

T cells...

_____

_____

_____

Bone marrow cannot...

_____

_____

_____

Opportunistic diseases...

_____

_____

_____

→ **AIDS**

Vocabulary Check

2. HIV stands for *human immunodeficiency virus.* The second word contains the root words *immune* and *deficiency.* How can these two words help you to remember the definition of HIV?

_____

_____

3. What does AIDS stand for, and how does the last word, beginning with "s," help you to remember that it is a disease and not a virus?

_____

_____

4. How does the word *opportunity* help you remember the definition of *opportunistic infection?*

_____

_____

NUTRIENTS AND HOMEOSTASIS
| **Study Guide**

KEY CONCEPT
Cells require many different nutrients.

MAIN IDEA: Six types of nutrients help to maintain homeostasis.

Fill in the concept map to summarize what you know about the six nutrients.

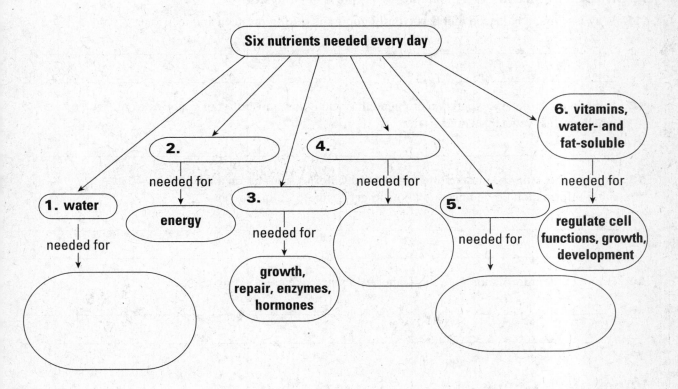

7. Many dietary experts recommend drinking about 8 glasses of water a day. Why do you need this much fluid to maintain homeostasis?

_____

_____

8. Explain why vegans, who eat no animal products, might have difficulty obtaining all 8 essential amino acids from their diet.

_____

_____

9. What is the difference between saturated and unsaturated fats?

_____

_____

10. Which of the six nutrients supply the body with energy?

_____

MAIN IDEA: **Meeting nutritional needs supports good health.**

11. Why is eating a balanced diet particularly important during pre-teen and teen years?

_____

_____

12. Why do most dietary experts recommend that you obtain most of your Calories from whole grains, vegetables, and fruits?

_____

13. You are checking the number of Calories and Calories from fat on a food label. What other information do you need to know to get accurate Calorie counts?

_____

_____

14. How can the information on a food label help you make good eating choices?

_____

_____

Vocabulary Check

15. The words *calorie* and *Calorie* both refer to a unit of energy. What is the difference in meaning between these two words?

_____

_____

16. The Latin term *vita* means "life." How does this meaning relate to the function of vitamins?

_____

_____

SECTION 32.2 | DIGESTIVE SYSTEM
Study Guide

KEY CONCEPT

The digestive system breaks down food into simpler molecules.

VOCABULARY		
digestion	esophagus	chyme
digestive system	peristalsis	small intestine
sphincter	stomach	bile

MAIN IDEA: Several digestive organs work together to break down food.

1. What is the main function of digestion?

_____

_____

2. Give an example of mechanical and chemical digestion.

_____

_____

3. How do smooth muscles and sphincters keep food moving in one direction throughout the digestive system?

_____

_____

4. What happens after digestion is completed?

_____

_____

MAIN IDEA: Digestion begins in the mouth and continues in the stomach.

5. Fill in the chart below to help you remember facts about key digestive enzymes.

Enzyme	Function
salivary amylase, amylase	
pepsin, peptides	
lipase	

CHAPTER 32
Digestive and Excretory Systems

MAIN IDEA: Digestion is completed in part of the small intestine.

Fill in the process diagram below to summarize the digestion of food as it moves through the mouth, stomach, and small intestine. Use Figure 32.11 to help you.

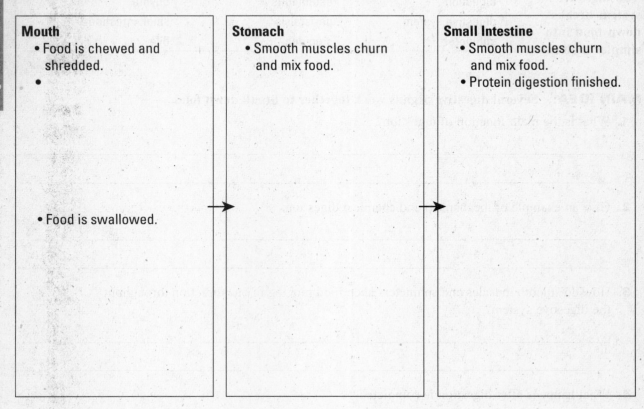

Mouth
- Food is chewed and shredded.
-

- Food is swallowed.

Stomach
- Smooth muscles churn and mix food.

Small Intestine
- Smooth muscles churn and mix food.
- Protein digestion finished.

6. What keeps the stomach from digesting itself?

_____

_____

Vocabulary Check

7. The word *esophagus* is based on the Greek terms *ois-*, which refers to "carrying something," and *phagos*, which means "food." How can these Greek terms help you remember the meaning of *esophagus*?

_____

8. Think of an analogy that might help you to explain the meaning of *peristalsis* to someone who does not know the word.

_____

_____

SECTION 32.3 | ABSORPTION OF NUTRIENTS
Study Guide

KEY CONCEPT
Nutrients are absorbed and solid wastes eliminated after digestion.

VOCABULARY	
absorption	microvilli
villi	

MAIN IDEA: Most absorption of nutrients occurs in the small intestine.

1. What is absorption, and why is it important to your body?

_____

_____

2. Name the three structures in the small intestine that absorb most of the nutrients from chyme.

_____

3. How do these three structures increase the surface area of the small intestine?

_____

_____

4. Why is it important that food move slowly through the small intestine?

_____

5. Fill in the chart summarizing absorption in the three parts of the small intestine.

Part of Small Intestine	Materials Absorbed	Distribution
duodenum		
		circulatory system
	fat-soluble vitamins, vitamin B_{12}, fatty acid, cholesterol, some water	

6. What happens when nutrient-rich blood leaves the small intestine and enters the liver?

_____

_____

MAIN IDEA: **Water is absorbed and solid wastes are eliminated from the large intestine.**

7. How does the large intestine help to maintain the body's fluid balance, or homeostasis?

_____

8. What materials make up the feces?

_____

_____

9. In what ways can bacteria in the large intestine be helpful or harmful?

_____

_____

_____

10. How is solid waste eliminated from the body?

_____

_____

Vocabulary Check

11. The Latin word *villus* means "shaggy hair," and *micro* refers to something that is unusually small. How can these two terms help you remember the meaning of *microvilli*?

_____

_____

12. Draw a sketch or think of an analogy to illustrate the meaning of *absorption*. Think of times you have watched water or other liquids being absorbed by something.

SECTION
32.4 | EXCRETORY SYSTEM
Study Guide

KEY CONCEPT
The excretory system removes wastes and helps maintain homeostasis.

VOCABULARY		
excretory system	urinary bladder	dialysis
kidney	nephron	
ureter	glomerulus	

MAIN IDEA: The excretory system eliminates nonsolid wastes and helps maintain homeostasis.

1. What are the main organs of the excretory system?

_____

_____

2. Name three ways that the excretory system eliminates nonsolid wastes.

_____

3. What are the waste products removed by the lungs?

_____

MAIN IDEA: The kidneys help to maintain homeostasis by filtering the blood.

4. What are the main parts of the kidney?

_____

_____

5. The kidneys release key hormones to help maintain homeostasis. In what other ways do the kidneys help to maintain homeostasis?

_____

_____

_____

MAIN IDEA: Nephrons clean the blood and produce urine.

6. What are the main functions of the glomerulus and Bowman's capsule?

_____

_____

Section 32.4 STUDY GUIDE CONTINUED

CHAPTER 32
Digestive and Excretory Systems

Fill in the process diagram to summarize the three steps in which blood is filtered and urine is formed in the nephron.

Filtration	Reabsorption	Excretion
• Blood enters glomerulus • Small molecules diffuse into Bowman's capsule, forming filtrate		

MAIN IDEA: **Injury and disease can damage the kidneys.**

7. How can diabetes and high blood pressure affect the kidneys?

_____

_____

8. How is the process of dialysis similar to the function of the kidneys?

_____

_____

Vocabulary Check

9. Which vocabulary words are based on the verbs *excrete* and *urinate*?

_____

10. *Dialysis* is based on the Greek word *dialuein,* which means "to break apart." What "breaking apart" does a dialysis machine do?

_____

_____

SECTION
33.1
SKELETAL SYSTEM
Study Guide

KEY CONCEPT

The skeletal system includes bones and tissues that are important for supporting, protecting, and moving your body.

VOCABULARY		
skeletal system	vertebrae	ligament
appendicular skeleton	cartilage	calcification
axial skeleton	joint	

MAIN IDEA: Your skeletal system is made up of the appendicular and axial skeletons.

1. What does the skeletal system do?

_____

Fill in the concept map to take notes on the parts of the skeletal system.

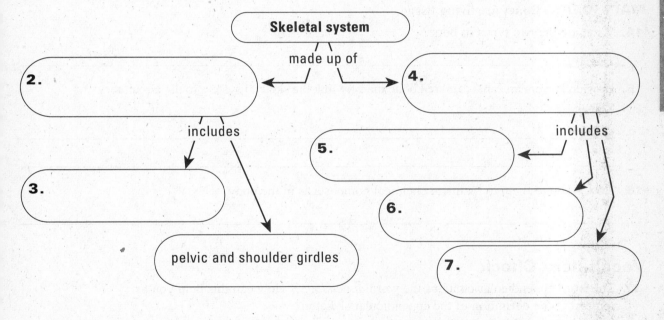

8. What is the function of the vertebrae?

_____

9. How is cartilage different from bone?

_____

_____

Section 33.1 STUDY GUIDE CONTINUED

MAIN IDEA: Bones connect to form joints.

10. What is a joint?

_____

11. What two places in the body are cartilaginous joints found?

_____

12. How do ligaments work to allow synovial joints to move?

_____

13. What are the five types of synovial joints?

_____

MAIN IDEA: Bones are living tissue.

14. What are the two types of bone?

_____

15. How do Haversian canals and red bone marrow link the skeletal system to the circulatory system?

_____

_____

16. How do bones help to maintain chemical homeostasis in the body?

_____

Vocabulary Check

17. The word appendicular contains the word *appendages*. How can this help you to remember the definition of the appendicular skeleton?

_____

18. The word axial contains the word *axis*. Knowing this, define what the axial skeleton is.

_____

19. The prefix *calci-*, which means "calcium," is found in the vocabulary word *calcification*. How can this clue help you to remember the definition of calcification?

_____

20. What are two things that cartilage, joints, and ligaments all have in common?

_____

CHAPTER 33
Protection, Support, and Movement

KEY CONCEPT

Muscles are tissues that can contract, enabling movement.

VOCABULARY			
muscular system	tendon	myofibril	myosin
muscle fiber	smooth muscle	sarcomere	
skeletal muscle	cardiac muscle	actin	

MAIN IDEA: Humans have three types of muscle.

Use the chart, and Figure 33.7 in your book, to organize your notes on the three different types of muscle.

Type of Muscle	Attaches to/Found in	Moves	Voluntary or Involuntary?
1. Skeletal			
2. Smooth			
3. Cardiac			

MAIN IDEA: Muscles contract when the nervous system causes muscle filaments to move.

4. What shortens when a muscle is contracted?

_____

5. Which filament is anchored to the middle of the sarcomere?

_____

6. Which filament is anchored to the Z line?

_____

7. Where is the Z line located?

_____

8. What stimulates a muscle contraction?

_____

9. How is calcium ion (Ca^{2+}) important for muscle contraction?

_____

In the space below, draw two diagrams: one of a relaxed sarcomere, and the second of a contracted sarcomere. Label actin, myosin, Z line, M line, and sarcomere in your drawings.

Relaxed

Contracted

10. What happens to actin and myosin when muscles relax?

_____

Vocabulary Check

11. On each of the lines below, write one of the three types of muscles and say where that type is found.

_____

_____

_____

12. Write two sentences or clues, one for each word, that will help you remember the difference between actin and myosin. (Example: Actin is *acti*vely pulled.)

_____

INTEGUMENTARY SYSTEM
Study Guide

KEY CONCEPT

The integumentary system has many tissues that protect the body.

VOCABULARY		
integumentary system	epidermis	hair follicle
keratin	dermis	

MAIN IDEA: The integumentary system helps maintain homeostasis.

1. What is the integumentary system?

_____

2. What are the two main functions of the integumentary system?

_____

3. How does the integumentary system prevent infection?

_____

MAIN IDEA: The integumentary system consists of many different tissues.

In the space below, draw and label all of the important structures within the skin.

Section 33.3 STUDY GUIDE CONTINUED

Layer of Skin	Structures It Contains	Function
4. epidermis		
5. dermis		
6. subcutaneous fat		

7. What are the functions of keratin and melanin?

_____

_____

8. What in the dermis gives the skin structure and flexibility?

_____

Vocabulary Check

9. The prefix *epi-* means above. How does this help you to remember the difference between the dermis and the epidermis?

_____

_____

10. Write a clue to help you remember what keratin is. It could be a rhyme, an analogy, or something entirely different.

_____

_____

11. Hair and hair follicles are different structures. The word *follicle* means "cavity of cells." How can knowing this help you to remember what a hair follicle is?

_____

_____

REPRODUCTIVE ANATOMY
Study Guide

KEY CONCEPT

Female and male reproductive organs fully develop during puberty.

VOCABULARY			
reproductive system	uterus	testosterone	semen
puberty	estrogen	scrotum	
ovum	fallopian tube	epididymis	
ovary	testis	vas deferens	

MAIN IDEA: The female reproductive system produces ova.

1. What is the reproductive system?

_____

_____

2. What hormones begin the process of puberty?

_____

3. What are the main functions of the female reproductive system?

_____

4. Name the three roles of the hormone estrogen in the female reproductive system.

_____

_____

_____

5. Describe the function of each part of the female reproductive system listed below.

Part of Reproductive System	Function
ovaries	
fallopian tube	
uterus	

Section 34.1 STUDY GUIDE CONTINUED

MAIN IDEA: **The male reproductive system produces sperm.**

6. What are the main functions of the male reproductive system?

_____

_____

7. Name the two roles of the hormone testosterone in the male reproductive system.

_____

_____

8. Describe the function of each part of the male reproductive system listed below.

Part of Reproductive System	Function
testes	
epididymus	
vas deferens	

Vocabulary Check

epididymis	vas deferens	fallopian tube

9. Each of the terms listed above refer to tubes found in the human reproductive system. Come up with a clue that will help you to remember each word's definition and how the definition is different from the other two.

_____

_____

_____

_____

KEY CONCEPT

Human reproductive processes depend on cycles of hormones.

VOCABULARY		
follicle	endometrium	zygote
ovulation	corpus luteum	infertility
menstrual cycle	menopause	sexually transmitted disease

MAIN IDEAS: Eggs mature and are released according to hormonal cycles. Sperm production in the testes is controlled by hormones.

Answer the questions in the chart regarding both female and male reproductive cycles.

Question	Female	Male
1. What type of cell division produces mature eggs and sperm?		
2. At what stage of life does egg or sperm production begin?		
3. What hormones stimulate the cycle of egg or sperm production?		

4. What is the menstrual cycle?

_____

_____

5. How does the endometrium change during the three phases of the menstrual cycle?

_____

_____

MAIN IDEA: Fertilization occurs when a sperm cell joins an egg cell.

6. Out of millions of sperm, usually only one can fertilize an egg. Explain why.

_____

7. What happens genetically to produce a zygote?

_____

_____

8. What is the difference between identical and fraternal twins?

_____

CHAPTER 34
Reproduction and Development

9. List three reasons a person might become infertile.

_____

MAIN IDEA: **Sexually transmitted diseases affect fertility and overall health.**

10. What characteristic must a disease have for it to be a sexually transmitted disease?

_____

11. Use the table below to describe the different types of STDs, their effects on health, and their treatment.

Type of STD	Examples	Effects	Treatment
bacterial infections			
viral infections			

Vocabulary Check

12. The prefix *meno-* means "relating to menstruation," and *pause* means "to stop." How does this help you to remember the definition for the word *menopause?*

_____

13. How does knowing the definition of the word *transmitted* help you to remember what a *sexually transmitted disease* is?

_____

14. The prefix *in-* means "not." How can this be a clue to the meaning of the word *infertility?*

_____

KEY CONCEPT

Development progresses in stages from zygote to fetus.

VOCABULARY

blastocyst	placenta	fetus
embryo	umbilical cord	
amniotic sac	trimester	

MAIN IDEA: The fertilized egg implants into the uterus and is nourished by the placenta.

1. What is the difference between a blastocyst and an embryo?

_____

_____

2. Fill in the following chart to summarize what you know about the structures that nourish and protect the growing embryo.

Structure	Description and Functions
amniotic sac	
chorion	
placenta	
umbilical cord	

3. Why must the blood flows of the mother and the embryo be kept separate?

_____

_____

MAIN IDEA: **A zygote develops into a fully formed fetus in about 38 weeks.**

4. In the first trimester of human life, what are some of the major organs that are forming and beginning to function?

_____

5. Would a mother be more likely to feel the fetus moving in the first trimester or in the second trimester? Explain your answer.

_____

_____

6. Why would a fetus who is born at the beginning of the third trimester have a difficult time surviving?

_____

MAIN IDEA: **The mother affects the fetus and the pregnancy affects the mother.**

7. Why is the quality of the mother's diet so important to the developing fetus?

_____

_____

8. Besides proper diet, what else can the mother do to help ensure a heathy pregnancy for herself and her baby?

_____

9. How can fluctuating hormone levels affect the mother's health during and just after a pregnancy?

_____

Vocabulary Check

10. In the space below, draw a sketch that illustrates the terms *amniotic sac, placenta,* and *umbilical cord.* You can use Figure 34.10 as a reference or think up your own example, such as an astronaut's suit.

SECTION
34.4 | BIRTH AND DEVELOPMENT
Study Guide

KEY CONCEPT
Physical development continues through adolescence and declines with age.

MAIN IDEA: **Birth occurs in three stages.**

Fill in the cause-and-effect chart about the birth process, showing that one cause can have multiple effects.

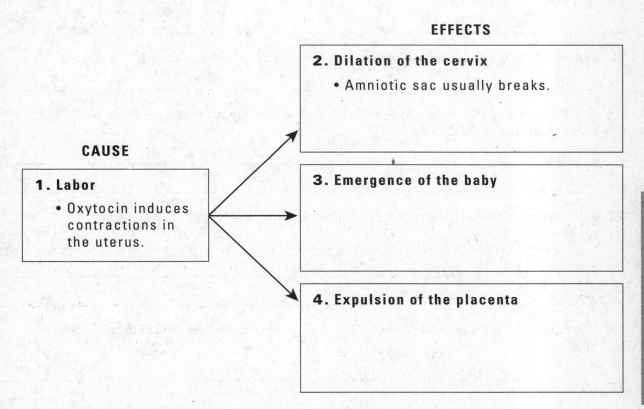

EFFECTS

CAUSE

1. Labor
  • Oxytocin induces contractions in the uterus.

2. Dilation of the cervix
  • Amniotic sac usually breaks.

3. Emergence of the baby

4. Expulsion of the placenta

5. If the cervix does not dilate enough, how is the baby removed from the mother?

_____

_____

6. What happens to the umbilical cord after the baby is born?

_____

MAIN IDEA: Human growth and aging also occur in stages.

7. What is the effect of the human growth hormone (hGH) on the body?

_____

_____

8. What are the main stages of development in human life after birth?

_____

9. Why might an infant's heart rate, breathing rate, and body temperature vary more than they do in older children?

_____

10. During which two stages of development does the greatest growth rate occur?

_____

11. What might be one reason that most children learn to walk around the end of infancy or the beginning of childhood?

_____

_____

12. List some of the major changes that occur in adolescence.

_____

_____

_____

13. What are some of the activities that can help to slow down or counteract the effects of aging?

_____

Vocabulary Check

14. The suffix *-hood* refers to "a group sharing a specific state or quality." How does this meaning relate to the terms *childhood* and *adulthood*?

_____

15. The word *adolescence* is based on the Latin verb *adolescere*, which means "to grow up." How does this help you understand the definition of *adolescence*?

_____

_____